PRAIRIE STORIES

MIKE AMOS

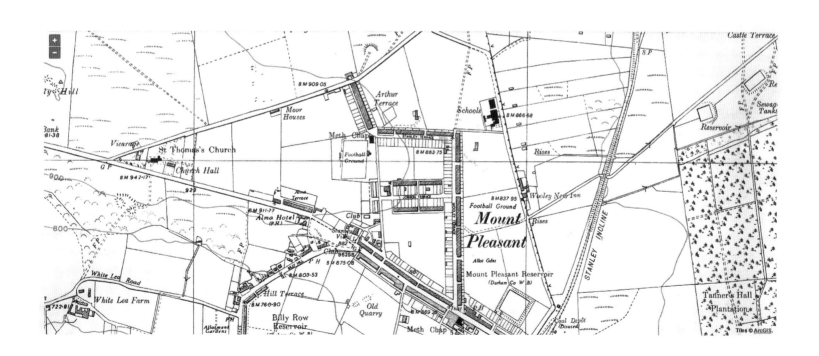

For Sharon, with whom the
view is always better

Published by Mike Amos
8 Oakfelds, Middleton Tyas, Richmond, North Yorkshire
Email mikeamos81@aol.com
Blog www.mikeamosblog.wordpress.com

Designed and typeset by County Print
using Adobe InDesign and Adobe Photoshop.
Text set in 11pt Times New Roman.
Printed by County Print, 11 Collingwood Court, Riverside
Park Industrial Estate, Middlesbrough TS2 1RP
01642 225867
sales@countyprint.co.uk

Most of the illustrations in this book have been used with kind
permission of the If you lived at Stanley Crook Facebook
Group and The Northern Echo. If any other illustration is
in copyright but not been acknowledged, the author will be
grateful for information and will happily make amends in
future editions.

ISBN:
978-1-8380404-2-0

Contents

Prologue

Surveys, sometimes spurious, suppose journalists to be the country's second-least trustworthy profession. Estate agents – begging their pardon – usually come top, with politicians and pollisses clustered in the frame.

Since I was a professional journalist for 55 years, it's probably best to begin with a confession, an attempt at reader reassurance: the prologue is almost the last thing in *Prairie Stories* to be written, and not quite the ultimate only because there has to be an epilogue as well.

There's also a good story about me and the epilogue back in the black-and-white days when it was a nightly five-minute God slot on Tyne Tees Television, but that's been told elsewhere.

A further confession would concede that I'm neither historian nor geographer, not archivist, anthropologist or sociologist. So what's it all about, and why a 60,000-word book on Stanley Hill Top?

Truth to tell – what else? - the book began with three aims, perhaps the primary purpose to provide a snapshot of life and times, past and present, in what may have been a fairly typical Co Durham pit village, and fairly gently to wonder whether or not things have changed for the better. The hope was to offer a fairly light touch, an entertainment not an education, though some unexpectedly dark clouds will gather. The book seeks to be nothing more than a nine-month chronicle, the conception planned but the gestation period almost accidental.

The secondary aims were to mark the end of the most constraining of Covid's lockdowns and to occupy my dangling days, emptier since *The Northern Echo* ended my employment in November 2019. An autobiography, where the story of the epilogue may be found, had first helped fulfil that end.

Others talk rather righteously of their "not-for-profit" enterprises. We self-published authors expect nothing else, hopeful that the venture might break even but mildly astonished were it ever to happen.

I'm a Co Durham lad – Shildon, which may just crop up once or twice in the coming pages – and very proud of that fact. Though long familiar with the smaller of the county's two Stanleys, and very fond of the old place, the association was chiefly through Stanley United FC and their regally ramshackle little ground, long known to my *Echo* readers as The Little House on the Prairie. Hence the book's title, hence the picture on the cover.

Nor could the village's reputation for being a bit on the fresh side be ignored. How might they keep the home fires burning when there's no concessionary coal? Other questions also arose. How might you retain a colliery camaraderie when you're not all in it, up to the oxters, together? Can old and new harmoniously co-habit, if not necessarily be joined together in holy matrimony? How might social intercourse be encouraged when there's no longer a pub, nor even a corner shop? Has the transplant taken?

Those who know the glorious County Palatine will also appreciate that the two Stanleys are oft confused, the Hill Top haven much the more scenic. Best efforts notwithstanding, big brother keeps butting into the account (and the swingers' club is definitely one of theirs.)

Another dark cloud, over Stanley and another 120 Co Durham villages for more than two decades until the mid-70s, was

Durham County Council's scandalously short-sighed and obstinately advocated Category D policy, which condemned places like the Hill Top to a slow death. How has it survived the reprieve?

All that's beginning to sound a bit pious; pompous, even. It's not the intention. The book which follows is primarily intended to entertain. Trust me, I'm a journalist.

Mike Amos MBE

March 2022

1: Spring fervour

March 31 2021

The Wind in the Willows, it may be recalled, begins with Mole giving his subterranean front parlour its annual whitewash – "working very hard all morning" – and not best pleased about it, either.

"Spring was moving in the air above and in the earth around and beneath him," wrote Kenneth Grahame. "penetrating even his lowly little house with its spirit of divine discontent and longing."

Finally, of course, old Moley downs tools, cries "Bother" and "Oh blow" and hares heliotropically towards the mad March sun.

Today's a bit like that.

It's the third day of a further gentle easing of lockdown's Covid-constrained chains, yesterday the hottest March day since Fred Fahrenheit was a nipper and this morning barely a shiver beneath.

Bank Top – Stanley in former times

No longer required to stay at home, rather to remain "local" – the interpretation of "local" may be a matter for another forum – we cry Freedom, to which "Bother" and "Oh blow" may be added according to taste, and head almost exultantly northwards up the A68.

For a year now, Sharon and I have obeyed the rules pretty strictly. Today there's a shaft of light and we're aiming for Stanley Hill Top, only about 30 miles north the furthest we've been these past 12 months. Stanley Hill Top has become the Wide World.

The notion of a book about Stanley – formally Stanley Crook, formerly Mount Pleasant, perhaps Wooley Terrace or simply just Wooley – occurred amid interminable months of winter quarters confinement, chiefly as an aid to sanity. Readers may in due course judge if the therapy were successful.

The title is a nod to Stanley United's wondrous, quirky and passionately loved little football ground, where once stood a gloriously higgledy-piggledy pavilion, whitewashed and ever-welcoming, known to readers of my *Northern Echo* columns – and to football followers nationwide – as "The Little House on the Prairie"

Coal fired as insatiably as one of Messrs Pease and Co's more voracious blast furnaces, the Little House offered shelter to players and spectators alike from all that Stanley's infamously Arctic micro-climate might headlong hurl at them. It was perhaps bitterly ironic that local ne'er-do-wells should burn the dear place down.

County Durham may be thought to have two Stanleys, the other 20-or-so miles to the north and much larger, both names thought to come from the Old English "stony clearing." *Bartholomew's Gazetteer* lists ten in the UK plus another 16 places with Stanley as part of their name. None of them is Accrington Stanley. Accrington Stanley's a different story altogether.

First published in 1953, Arthur Mee's acclaimed *Durham* – by which was meant the County Palatine, between Tyne and Tees – failed to mention Stanley Hill Top at all. It may be little consolation, or perhaps a source of schadenfreude, that (West) Stanley, the one up the road, was wholly overlooked as well.

Wikipedia reckons the wide world to have 38 places called Stanley, 23 of them in the United States, three in Australia and the others ranging from the Falklands Islands (perhaps the second most famous) to Mauritius and from Hong Kong to the North Mariana Islands. In the course of compiling, December 2021, a potential reader spotted a headline that Stanley was applying to become a city and became quite excited at the prospect.

Sadly the small print talked of Port Stanley, that Falkland outpost where we battled with the Argentinians. Wasn't the governor general from Redcar?

Wiki in turn supposes the UK to have just four Stanleys – and here's another problem. They're listed in Derbyshire, Wakefield, Perth and Kinross and Co Durham – not the fascinating little village to which this book is dedicated but the big brother flagged up in the prologue and mentioned a couple of paragraphs ago. Suffice that "our" Stanley must formally be suffixed – Crook, Hill Top, heaven alone knows - though to most it simply remains Stanley.

Home to about 450 folk when someone last counted, probably

Crowning glory – Coronation carnival 1953

more when the new census is totted up, it's exposed atop a Windy Ridge a couple of vertiginous miles above Crook and 1,000 feet above the ocean. In the 1950s and for two decades afterwards it was among 121 villages doomed by Durham County Council's obdurately asinine Category D policy to a slow "no development" death.

It had been a pit village, of course, and, mercifully, evinced the colliers' resilience. Much more of Stanley's collieries in due course.

So for gloomy months I've chipped away at the internet, written a few emails, longed like the Mole to burrow from the darkness, to talk to people, to cry "Bother" and "Oh blow" and, simply, to get up to Stanley and to join in. Up on North Tyneside, Ray Ion has also been ferreting cheerfully and diligently on my behalf and his contributions will several times be acknowledged.

Right Honourable – Ernest Armstrong

Today's the day, today's getting on 70 degrees in old money. Today's not just a new chapter, but a new beginning, and it wouldn't in the least be surprising if a wise old Water Rat poked its head from the verge by way of vernal greeting.

We park on High Road – Stanley was never likely to have a Low Road – next to the fabled football ground and to where the happy, harvest-homely little Wooley Terrace Methodist chapel once witnessed for Mr Wesley.

Chapel folk, it might be added, rhymed "Wooley" with "truly". Others prefer the sound of a double knit jumper. Sides may have to be taken before the page count's complete.

I'd attended Harvest Festival there in 2008, traditional altar rail offerings augmented by a tin of peaches (in light syrup), a can of Asda baked beans, a couple of jars of home-made bramble jam – had it not been home-made, it would have been called blackberry – and a few nick-nacks from the woodworking group which met in the little vestry out the back. If this were the harvest table, then Wooley Terrace was in a promotion place.

The chapel had little changed down the years, though – like much of the rest of the village – it had gained a WC. "We used to have to send the preacher to the earth closet out the back," said Doreen Ainsley, the steward. "It didn't seem right."

About 15 were present, few (if any) under pensionable age, the baked beans a reminder of one of the revered Archbishop Desmond Tutu's favourite graces: "We thank thee Lord for beans on toast, Father, Son and Holy Ghost." The rest of the village, it seemed, had ploughed the fields and scattered. The chapel closed soon afterwards.

The name which this morning resonates most clearly in the springtime silence is that of the late Ernest Armstrong, combative footballer and good Methodist, who became MP for NW Durham, government minister, deputy Speaker of the

FRANCIS STREET, WOOLEY TERRACE, CROOK

Shop early...

Commons and vice-president of the Methodist Conference – highest office open to a layman – but who on the Hill Top is remembered simply as Sikey.

On the football field Ernest was reckoned a resolute defender, what euphemists call uncompromising, and maybe a bit short-sighted, too. It might have explained that shocking tackle on the referee.

The chapel's gone, sacrificed to housing, The football ground – identified on an 1895 map as the Methodist Chapel football ground – remains, abandoned, still bordered on the High Road side by the sort of wall over which only a 7ft skinflint would be able to peer without forswearing parsimony and paying his sixpence at the gate.

A set of redundant goalposts still somehow stands, askance, as on the far side does what football folk term a scratching shed stand, listing if not listed and perhaps about to resume the poultry-keeping purposes its name suggests.

There've been no footballers since 2005. "I don't care if it's Gurney Valley Salmon Can Dribblers who use the ground," former club chairman Vince Kirkup had famously said, "so long as they change their name to Stanley United." Only horses play there now, and not even with an empty tin of John West's with which to kick about.

On a fence at the back of the Aged Miners' Homes, immediately adjoining the ground, someone – possibly an aged miner, though he'd have to be a *very* aged miner – has hung out his proggy mats to dry in the spring sunshine, as probably the Mole would have done.

Another elderly chap salutes the day from the mobility scooter to which his dog is energetically attached. He wears a perky straw hat. "I've tekken off me jacket and then me jumper," he says though they've taken off no further than the back of the scooter.

You can't be too careful on Stanley Hill Top.

The post lady, too, goes about her business in shirt sleeves and shorts, a defiance of Royal Mail regulations which ordain ne'er to cast a clout till May is out (or, in Stanley, until St Swithin's Day, whichever is the later.)

Everyone's cheery, everyone's chatty. We're talkative in return. These are folk to whom I might yet have to try to sell a book and, right now, I'm warming to the theme.

So we essay an initial tour of the village, sun blessed and socially distanced, the first of goodness knows how many discursions in merry months to come. It may not be termed a fact-finding mission, of course, since these days that's much easier by Internet.

It was on the Internet, the first tentative morning of exploration, that on a website called *I Live Here*, I came across a supposed summary of life on the Hill Top, as vacuous as it was vicious. "It's not populated by anyone really, unless you count the odd dead sheep and knackered 300-year-old terraced houses. Unfortunately they only knocked down a couple of streets before disappearing back to civilisation.

"The result is a barren collection of streets on a bleak hill with internet served weekly on the back of a horse and cart and no shops within two days walk. No one in their right mind lives here or anywhere closely near here. The only thing remotely interesting about Stanley is the view."

To find somewhere more agreeable to live, the account added, settlers should head 100 miles east and find a rock in the middle of the North Sea.

It may not be too much of a pre-judgement, what folk now like to call a spoiler, to suggest that I'm unlikely to agree.

The wind turbines are immobile, perhaps breathless in astonishment, perhaps checking the calendar to ascertain that it really is still just March. Daffs dally, larrikin lambs wonder what all the fuss was about. Bairns defer, perhaps because they're as well brought up as the village school's Ofsted report unequivocally and enthusiastically suggests, perhaps simply because they remember their pandemic protocols.

Only an inordinate number of police sirens threatens the serenity. Already, unsurprisingly, they may know something that I don't.

In St Thomas's wooded churchyard, on the village's western extremity, many of the heart-shaped memorials suggest that those whose passing they mark may have died elsewhere than in their beds. They were much too young.

One memorial is to a seven-year-old girl who died from "accidental" burns, another commemorates Sydney George Bell, aged just 13 years and eight months when he died in 1909:

You must not cry, my parents dear

And want me back again.

But think how sweet it will be for me

To suffer no more pain.

Another memorial is to Mary Jane Clark, aged just 37, and to her month-old daughter:

Farewell my husband and children dear,

I've toiled for you for many a year.

I've struggled long to do my best

And now I've gone to take my rest.

I've several times over the years attended services at St Thomas's, where the laid-up Wooley Terrace colliery banner enjoins to "Succour the widows and orphans" and where, in the early 21st century, the priest-in-charge was Fr Peter Davis, an agreeable Australian monk who, too briefly, swept through those parts like the Blizzard of Oz.

Pleasant spot, 1855

Peter was also vicar of Tow Law, where he lived, a community a couple of miles to the west but not a string vest warmer. Poor Friar Tucker swore that all that sustained him was a larder stocked floor to ceiling with Campbell's lobster bisque and Fray Bentos steak and kidney pudding, admittedly admirable choices. His medicine cupboard, he'd add, would put Boots the Chemist to shame.

By way of reinforcing his point, Tow Law vicarage was reckoned the first in the Church of England to have double glazing.

Last I heard of Fr Peter, he was a buffet car manager on the West Coast main railway line, though whether the buffet sold Fray Bentos steak and kidney pudding (much less Campbell's lobster bisque) is a matter of much doubt.

I also greatly admire Dave Ayre – long-serving churchwarden, principled trades union official and indefatigable cyclist, hope to catch up with him before many more pages are turned but hear that he and his wife Doris are in a care home down the bank in Billy Row. Miner's son, Stanley resident for all but the first year of his life, Dave sufficiently understood the village's unpredictable weather conditions never, ever, to let his fire go out – a mission in which physically and metaphorically he succeeded quite wonderfully.

From the church gate, from what locally are called the Heights of Alma and from many other Hill Top vantages, the view southwards is stupendous, further testimony to the crassness of Category D, as myopic as it was misanthropic. An opening gambit, perhaps, but who – save for the website warrior earlier mentioned – might not want to live here?

The County Council eventually compelled to back pedal, the village now has much handsome new housing, one house so posh that there's a putting green out the front.

What soon becomes equally clear, however, is that Stanley Hill Top wouldn't win Co Durham's best kept village award, or even Crook's. Perhaps wind-assisted, litter abounds.

The long, mid-Victorian, terraced main street – Mount Pleasant on one side, Francis Street on the other, Co-operative Terrace yet to be extrapolated – is unavoidably more humble, though one house even has a nameplate. It's called Innisfree, perhaps after William Butler Yeats's celebrated poem The Lake Isle of Innisfree.

I will arise and go now, and go to Innisfree

And a small cabin build there, of clay and wattle made….

And I shall have some peace there, for peace is dropping slow.

Innisfree is also the name of a US/Korean cosmetics company. We take a few moments, Sharon and I, to ponder whether this little house in Francis Street is occupied by a gentleman with a literary inclination or by the UK agent for some Far Eastern face paint factory. We decide it's probably the former, though there's no sign of a lake.

In a little courtyard garden across the road, however, a smiling Bill and Ben the Flowerpot Men angle ever optimistically in a man made pond.

Another thing that's quickly noticeable about the Hill Top is that there are no longer any shops. There's a bespoke furniture place – "created by craftsmen" – and a long-established taxi office but nowhere to buy a pint of milk, a pork pie or a paper. A board outside the Foresters guest house, at the east end,

Snow go area – Stanley

announces that fish and chips will be available on Good Friday lunchtime. We're two days too early, unable even to pick up the scraps.

A compensation, perhaps, is that there's a pretty good bus service, particularly for those up and doing before about 7am, when to some destinations the day's only service departs. The Arriva X1, which meanders both discursively and deceptively between Darlington and Tow Law, is happily much more frequent.

So the stroll continues. The village hall, still out of bounds, is decked with the sort of radio antennae which suggests that hams hang here but which in other circumstances might have seen service on the *Bismarck*. The Easter holidaying school, well out of the village, has been subject of rather more lockdown homework.

Its mission statement's prominent on the fence outside – "To try our best, to tell the truth, to look after each other and the community". An extract from the latest Ofsted report is similarly displayed – "Pupils' personal development and welfare is outstanding."

Insatiable and notorious grammarian, I'd personally give them an extra mark just for that correct use of the pesky possessive apostrophe,

All of it raises as many questions among itinerant oldies as it might with an inquisitive eight-year-old, and not just about where the pitmen toiled. Why is the school so far from the village? Will the head let me spend a day there? Do "old" and "new" Stanley live harmoniously cheek by jowl? Will the county council allow much more new housing? Could the vil-

lage sustain it? Who has the big house with the putting green, or finds peace at Innisfree? Will St Thomas's, without a Sunday service for more than a year, ever again hold one? As the patron saint might have supposed, it seems a matter of doubt.

We're just going to have to come back again, whenever patience and pandemic allow. Windy Ridge is a breath of fresh air.

2: everything in the garden....

April 28 2021

So this is what they mean by ne'er casting a clout. The thermometer on the Hill Top trembles on six degrees, the squally rain's colder than that.

There's a smell not of spring in the air but of wood glue, Staples Woodcraft presumably, though no warming sign of smoking chimneys. That we're gathered in Geoff Waterston's summerhouse, at the end of a truly secret (and very special) garden is evidence not of one or more swallows but of continuing coronavirus caution.

Geoff was in farming, reckons that Stanley has 60 fewer growing days annually than Durham City, a dozen or so miles northeast. "Growing days are when it's six degrees or over, that's when grass will grow. I read that in one of David Bellamy's books," he explains.

Today is International Workers' Memorial Day, marked globally every April 28 but perhaps seldom more passionately than in Stanley where traditionally a service is held at St Thomas's after a banner-bearing march along the village.

"Remember the dead, fight for the living," the watchword enjoins, though some – the radicals, no doubt – have been known to insert "like hell" between "fight" and "for".

On one occasion the organisers had rung the police – "purely out of courtesy," says Geoff – and were told that the march commemorating victims of industrial accidents couldn't be held for fear of accidents, health and safety and all that. It made the papers, even the telly. That year's preacher was a firebrand Methodist. "He said we should not only march to the church but march back again," Geoff adds.

Until a couple of years ago the chief organiser, chief motivator, chief whip was the magnificent Dave Ayre, now nearly 90 and recently – as the first chapter supposed – moved with Doris, his wife, to the West Lodge care home in Billy Row, about half a mile away, where creature comforts may be plenteous but probably don't include a coal fire.

I ring him from Geoff's. "I'm fine," Dave insists and we arrange to reunite as soon as restrictions allow. I greatly hope that it can happen.

That there was no Workers' Memorial Day at St Thomas's last year was because of Covid, the pandemic and Dave's indis-

Garden party - Johnathan Kindleysides,
Pam Oliver, Geoff Waterston

position making it again impossible today. That there may not be a service in coming years is because St Thomas's may no longer be open.

Usually the Sunday morning gathering is no more than four or five. "There's Vera, Dave and Doris, me and Pam," says Geoff. Pam Oliver is Dave's fellow churchwarden and Geoff's soul-mate, taking little part in the summerhouse session for shielding reasons.

She'd begun regularly attending church after 9/11, when others might have supposed that God had taken an extended furlough or at least, as the hymnist supposes, that He moves in a (very) mysterious way.. "Pam thought it was exactly when people needed Him," says Geoff..

Dave Ayre had said back in 2008 that it was important to keep the church open even if only one person came – "even if it's just to sit in the quiet and listen to the birds" – a notion with which Geoff agrees in principle but questions in practice. "The Church of England is about footfall and ours isn't big enough.

"We get full at Christmas, even though it's known to be a cold church, and we've had some fantastic events with great support from the village. They want it for weddings and funerals, they just don't want to come on Sunday mornings."

The International Workers' Memorial Day service has attracted at least four Bishops of Durham, past or present, never more memorably than when the late Dr David Jenkins, then 80 and retired to Teesdale, pitched up on the Hill Top.

Dr Jenkins was on fine and fiery fettle, still sawing the air like a mystic master carpenter. "Though in my 81st year and fed up of religious and religion, I can't for the life of me stop believing in God," he said.

"Today the most obvious and chief reason for not believing in God is the words and actions of those who say they do."

Church militant – Bishop David Jenkins

Geoff reckons that all the bishops did well – "even the ones we thought a bit right wing" – though some of the attendant brass bandsmen were less impressed. "Some said they wouldn't be coming back because it was too political. It did get a bit out-spoken, especially after Thatcher died. It's still a very good occasion, I really hope we can do it again."

Geoff and Pam have themselves a remarkable, even a romantic story. He'd spent the first three years of life in the other, much bigger and damn near ineluctable Stanley – West Stanley as locals still call it – moved with his parents to Newcastle and spent working years, pig exporting and breeding, somewhere down south.

In 1991 he returned north – "sort of semi-retired" – paying £7,000 to the National Coal Board for a 6.5 acre field near the former Weardale and Shildon Waterworks Company's reservoir on the Hill Top with the hope of keeping "a few" pigs. Few may now remember the Weardale and Shildon Waterworks Company, save that the Water House – one of Messrs Wetherspoons pubs in Durham City – now overflows its former head office.

Soon afterwards he bought a house in Railway Terrace, backing onto his field. Not long after that the end-terrace house next door also came on the market, bought by Pam, recovering from a divorce. Incredibly, his new neighbour had also been his childhood neighbour in West Stanley and while it may not (yet!) be said that he has married the girl next door, he concedes that they are partners.

We're joined in the summerhouse, heater in full vigour, by Pam's 40-year-old son Jonathan Kindleysides, pronounced not as in kindness but in kindergarten, who's head of industry at the renowned Beamish Museum in north-west Durham where Michelle, his wife, is head of health and wellbeing.

He and his mum had moved to Oakenshaw, a couple of miles east, though he still attended Stanley school, dreaming even then of a job at Beamish, getting work experience there and studying history and archaeology at university.

Jonathan now lives in Annfield Plain, closer to the museum, but talks possessively and in the present tense of the Hill Top. "When we moved here there was no new housing at all, they were pulling them down not putting them up," he says.

Many residents, former miners, were decanted down the bank to Billy Row with the promise of free coals for life. The new bungalows had central heating. "I don't know if the council saw the irony," says Jonathan,

So how did the Labour controlled Durham County Council get away for so long with a policy that condemned working class families to live not where they'd been settled for generations but where authority ordained that they must?

"I think they were convinced that when the pits were gone, there was no reason for people to live here any longer," says Geoff. "It was the same with Witton Park and many other places. They just thought that they could tip people out into places like Peterlee and Newton Aycliffe and it would be all right, they'd be grateful."

Inevitably the community has changed, both socially and physically. "The late Billy Ayre used to say that it would take him an hour to walk from one end of the street to the other, so many people sitting on their doorsteps, having a smoke, wanting to talk," says Geoff.

I'd met Billy Ayre, then 83, at the Wooley Terrace harvest festival back in 2008. "I remember this chapel when they had to open the partitions and still had to have chairs down all the aisles," he said. "Mind, it was much social as religious back then."

Geoff recalls his early days on the Hill Top, walking the dog. "I got to know quite a lot of people, good people, that way." One of the first was Keith Ayre, Dave's brother, a renowned local artist who'd spend holidays with his brother near Braemar, in Scotland.

"They're both republicans but one time Keith bumped into

the Duchess of Cornwall, I think they'd both slipped out for a smoke," says Geoff. "They were getting on really well until the security came rushing over."

Folk don't sit on their doorsteps any longer, he says, nor do many have allotments on which not just to grow prize veg but to put the world to rights. "It's a commuter village now. They go off to work in Durham or somewhere, come home at five o'clock and switch on the television."

Perhaps, he muses, he should get another dog.

Geoff had given up pig farming after the 2001 foot and mouth outbreak, his herd unaffected but slaughtered, nonetheless. He became a porter and a union official at the University Hospital of North Durham, retired again, went back when the pandemic began.

"I didn't venture up to the field for six months after that. It was quite traumatic," he says. Now those six-and-a-half acres are a glorious garden, still just with field grass, impossible to see and much less to imagine from the roadside out the front.

"It's Pam's work, really. I just dug a few holes," he insists.

"That's about it," says Pam.

Cultivation's not much helped by the weather, of course, global warming still taking its time to reach Stanley or to level up with Durham. "We've still been cut off a few times, but not for long," says Jonathan, almost defensively.

"The wind's the worst," says Geoff. "Every north window in the church has been blown out at one time or another. It's worse when the gale's from the south-west. There's nothing to stop it

until it gets to Stanley. There was one chap got a new house, lasted less than a year, couldn't stand it any longer.

"We enjoy living here for all that. It creeps up on you. I don't think we'll be going anywhere else now."

Duchess of Cornwall – quick fag?

3: Lady's day

May 18 2021

LNER, which runs today's train service to London – on Britain's railways, who knows what tomorrow might bring? – has a couple of times been in the news over the past week and on neither occasion would have welcomed the publicity.

The first story concerned problems with what might be called the undercarriage – Hitachi trains, built in Newton Aycliffe, services withdrawn – the second arose after the poor conductor had the effrontery over the PA to address passengers as "Ladies and gentlemen, boys and girls."

Not only did some twerp who identified as non-binary complain that it was offensive to people like them but, worse by far, LNER apologised and vowed that it wouldn't happen again.

It's the second day of the third stage of Boris's road map to Covid redemption. Perhaps at a loss over what to do for the best, the conductor on the 8 59 from Darlington restricts himself to "Hello". For reasons which cannot yet be imagined, the time may come when someone complains about that, an' all. Over-familiarity, perhaps.

I'm headed onward to Maze Hill station in the well-heeled London Borough of Greenwich, the area named after Sir Algernon May, a 17th century MP who lived there and was also from 1669-86 Keeper of the Records at the Tower of London. It's 30 easy-going minutes on South East Trains from St Pancras. The train's immaculate and uncrowded, the PA messages all automated. Sounds wise. You can't send an automaton on a diversity course, can you?

At Maze Hill I'm met by Hilary Armstrong, formally Baroness Armstrong of Hill Top – the Hill Top, being Stanley, of course - and formerly a local county councillor and MP for North West Durham. It's only later, however, that I discover that the formal list of honorary deputy lieutenants of Co Durham lists her as Baroness Armstrong of Toft Hill. The lieutenancy may need to look at a map.

Ernest Armstrong, her father – of whom readers have heard neither the first nor last – was himself the constituency member from 1964-87. His daughter, now 75, succeeded him. We are old friends.

As well as being Stanley United's centre half – remember Sikey? – Ernest became (as we were saying) deputy Speaker of the House of Commons, Vice-President of the Methodist Conference and, by no means least, president of the Northern Football League. He died in 1996. Hilary was parliamentary private secretary to John Smith when he led Her Majesty's opposition, became Labour Party chief whip – surprisingly hard-edged, it's said – during Tony Blair's tenure and is now chair of the Lords' Public Services committee, a role which she much enjoys.

For the past year or more she's been shielding, meetings held remotely – Zoom with a view – a return to joyful full vigour further threatened when she broke three ribs in a fall and by the appearance the following evening of her beloved Sunderland FC – beloved yet perfidious - against Lincoln City in the semi-final first leg of the English game's third tier play-offs.

A little Armstrong family gathering is planned in front of the television at the smart first floor apartment overlooking the Thames – wonderful views across the water to the sky-scraping City -where she lives with her husband, Dr Paul Corrigan CBE. Nothing on the walls or on the shelves suggests obvious memories of Stanley, though there's an imitation miner's lamp, a present from former Sunderland FC chairman Bob Murray.

"I had a real one," she says. "It was nicked."

There is, however, a photograph of The Strangers, a Coventry-based ska band which had seven successive top ten hits, including two No 1s, in the early 1980s. Though his successful career was in public service, Paul had a year as the band's manager.

He and Hilary also have a place in Seville. Culturally or climatically, that's probably not too much like Stanley, either.

Paul's a Londoner, West Ham fan by birth and by instinct but Sunderland supporter by marital default. "You have to, it's the rule," he says cheerfully. "When the wedding service speaks of 'for better for worse;, the worst is Sunderland."

Until Stanley United gave up the ghost in 2003, cause of death given as exhaustion and apathy, Hilary's football loyalties were divided, probably equally. Sundry other Armstrongs had in better times helped ensure that the team from the Little House on the Prairie punched, usually just figuratively, way above its weight.

Ernest – still figuratively, understand – punched harder than most. Why Sikey? "I think it was just because he was a hard nut," says his daughter.

In the Northern League until 1974 all teams – even the wonderfully successful ones like Bishop Auckland and Crook Town, both multiple winners of the FA Amateur Cup – were meant strictly to be amateur, paying only legitimate expenses. Surely United's players must have found a little something in their

boots at the end of the game, and not just a tube of Ralgex?

Hilary's briefly, unusually, defensive. "We didn't pay as much as Crook did," she says and glances briefly at her watch. It's not for the time – with which she's greatly generous – but to check her messages. Even on the first floor, things are pretty high tech.

In the 1994 book *Football and the Commons People*, accounts of their football allegiance by 30 MPs and a fund raiser for the Child Poverty Action Group, she'd recalled early Saturdays - frozen and formative, single minded but double wrapped – on the oft-bleak United ground. By then they lived on Wearside. Her dad – "I always thought of him as a bit of a scout" – would also pile several Sunderland-based players into the car alongside her.

"I loved those afternoons. Dark, cold and wet they may have been but I remember them with enormous pleasure, both because of the time spent with the family and because that is where my continuing passion for the game began," she wrote in 1994. "When Stanley took the field, I was out there with them: I lived every pass, ran for every ball and agonised over every missed opportunity."

Like father like daughter, she also admitted regularly having a go at the ref - "I think it's where I leaned to heckle," says Hilary – before seeking the sanctuary of the Little House, and the blaze of the great big coal fires – at the end of ninety nithered minutes.

"There's a family story that during a particularly bad tempered match the crowd invaded the pitch. My granddad was trying to get them off and my Uncle Dick was trying to get them back

Hill topper - Baroness Armstrong

on again."

On another occasion, still remembered up there, her cousin Jean married club captain Ronnie Tunstall, not just on a Saturday in the season but on a Saturday when United were facing the old enemy Crook Town, a couple of miles down the hill. The reception was in what Stanley folk called the Green Hut, but the groom and the male guests were quickly off to Crook.

So what did the young cousin do? "I was the bridesmaid, only about ten. I don't think I had any choice than to stop," she says.

Switching primary allegiance to Sunderland, standing with friends on the long-gone Roker End was, she supposes, an assertion of independence. Charlie Hurley was an early hero, then Dave Watson, another centre half. "I was still rather vocal, yelling and shouting at everyone," she'd written. "Whether encouragement of our players or abuse and vilification of the other team and the ref. I must have been an incredible pain in the neck."

So is she confident of a consoling Wednesday evening in front of the telly? "You know Sunderland," says Hilary. "We've been here before, haven't we?"

Ernest and Hannah, her parents, had moved to Sunderland before she was born but the story begins neither on the Hill Top nor in the lowlands by the Wear but in Brampton, Cumbria, where her great grandfather sired six sons and three daughters. Most were driven from home by their father's alcoholism. "I think there was a bit of abuse, too" says Hilary.

The men wandered the North-East from pit to pit, seeking work. John, her grandfather, pitched up at Wooley, variations in pronunciation previously noted. Interesting theory, Hilary supposes that the "truly" variant may have been preferred by those wary of being supposed Wooley backs.

It was her grandparents who became part of the founding generation of Methodists, a reaction – she's sure – to seeing at first hand the damage that drink at its most demonic could inflict. Neither smoked nor drank, both played an active part in the Primitive Methodist church in Stanley front street. "My grandmother in particular was very strong in the faith," says Hilary, whose parents became pillars of the Methodist movement in Sunderland and her father a local preacher.

Ernest was a teacher, became a headmaster, returned to Stanley with his family for school holidays, for merry Christmas and, of course, for the football. "Stanley was different," says Hilary. "I always felt that people were more friendly up there."

Though Primitive and Wesley factions had nationally united in 1932, Stanley's Methodists – like many more – continued to meet separately, perhaps suspiciously, for many years thereafter. Prims and proper, they'd tour Stanley's terraced streets with a portable harmonium, hymn singing on every corner, Sankey and Moody blues.

"My brother John and I were always recruited for the Sunday School anniversary, even though we lived in Sunderland, but I never remember going to Stanley and wishing I was somewhere else. Aunty Ethel spent weeks teaching them their party pieces but there was more than that. A lot of the kids would only learn to read and write properly at the Bible classes."

Hilary may also have become acclimatised. Her mother hadn't. "My dad was offered the headship of Sunniside school, the next village along, I think after the winter that the snow had

been up to the tops of the houses. My mum said she wasn't going to live there and that was that. You didn't have central heating, but they burned an awful lot of coal."

Aunty Ethel – everyone had an Aunty Ethel back then – ran a shop on the corner of Cooperative Terrace, selling everything from pop to paraffin. When the miners were hard up, Hilary recalls, they'd come in for a single Woodbine. Her Uncle Dick ran the village's newspaper business from his home. "All the men would gather on a Saturday night, waiting for the Pink to come. I'd just hang around with them; I loved the crack, especially about football. There's no doubt that the identity which came through the football was very important."

Her uncle John, the local representative on Durham County Council, was effectively in control of hand-outs to the desperately poor, the council having refused – despite threats of individual imprisonment – to means test under the Poor Law. "The money was kept in a big metal tea pot which he had in a cupboard next to the range where people cooked their food," says Hilary. "They knew everyone in the village. They'd know if anyone tried to take advantage of the situation. Very few did."

John died in 1945, from emphysema, having been encased in plaster to stop him coughing. She almost shudders as she recalls it.

She also remembers the colliery holidays when Wooley would close for two weeks, the pit ponies would be brought up for air – probably gasping for it, more of that later – and a dozen buses ("charabancs my Aunty Ethel called them") would line up to take pretty much the entire village to Blackpool, for what Stanley Holloway supposed fresh air and fun.

"I always wanted to know why we couldn't go, My dad would say 'You'll understand one day, pet'. He was right."

She'd been shortlisted for the vacant Sedgefield parliamentary seat in 1983 – losing out to the young Tony Blair – became county councillor for Crook North in 1985 and two years later held the seat which her father had so long kept warm, substantially increasing his majority. She stood down in 2010, elevated to the peerage soon afterwards. Ernest, inexplicably, never was.

Category D, which the Labour Party so long espoused? "I couldn't really get excited about it. It was a bit like levelling up, a lot of the old houses were dreadful. There are some really nice houses today."

The first suggestion was that she become Baroness Armstrong of Stanley Crook, an idea which little appealed to high authority because the title suggested not just ermine but vermin. "An unfortunate ring to it" said Garter King of Arms, the heraldic high-up responsible for such trimmings. The idea of Hill Top came – and not after a summit meeting, it should perhaps be made clear – in a letter from her cousin David, of whom more in the next chapter but one.

"We all knew what it meant" says Hilary. "It meant God's own country."

So why wasn't her distinguished father's parliamentary and public service marked with a life peerage? "It just didn't happen", she adds, perhaps disingenuously.

She walks back to Maze Hill station with me, down Pelton Road and past the Pelton Arms – both said to be named after an engineer from that part of Chester-le-Street who'd been instrumental in building Greenwich power station. Three days later both she and Paul will be headed back north, a four-day visit that because of the pandemic is the first for 15 months.

"There are an awful lot of folk we need to see," says Hilary. "It'll be great to be back, great to see Stanley. They're just such honest, decent people. I'll never tire of the Hill Top."

Before that, Sunderland go down 2-0 in the play-off at Lincoln City. There's always the second leg….

4: club trip

May 22 2021

In what some call the olden days, before about 1995, the working men of County Durham – and those of a more indolent disposition, too – could be seen hanging around outside the pubs and clubs, impatiently awaiting opening hour. Particularly, pre-prandially, it was a feature of Sunday dinner times.

New Year's Eve was different, and not just because the women folk might annually be allowed to join them. On New Year's Eve they formed a disorderly queue, an hour or more before the six o'clock start, lest the full house be not just restricted to the bingo.

I'm fearful of something a bit like that this evening, of hanging around outside Billy Row Club and the place not opening at all – or, indeed, ever opening again.

Billy Row is so seamlessly stitched to Stanley Hill Top that they seem damn near inseparable. Head down from Stanley main street and the fluorescent road sign – Billy Row – is at once in your face, up front and impersonal. Were it a defensive wall at a football match, a good referee would tell it to get back a bit or else face the consequences.

Early in the book's contemplation, I'd considered not mentioning Billy Row at all, partly because it seemed so aggressively territorial and partly because everywhere else would then want in on the act. In the mile-and-a-half or so between Crook and Stanley, communities oft overlapping, are Bank Foot, Peases West, Grahamsley, Roddymoor, White Lea, Billy Row and probably three or four I've forgotten or which have simply been misplaced. Mention one and you feel honour bound to mention all of them, and you could be on half the night.

Save for the somewhat apocryphal information that it was named after Sir William Row, and that it had 824 residents in the 2001 census, Billy Row's Google page is wholly unforthcoming. Other websites are little more helpful.

One site supposes that the club is open 24 hours a day seven days a week but prudently adds that times may vary. Another offers precisely the same information but suggests that things could be affected by Covid-19.

"24/7?" echoes Trevor Smith, the club's affable owner. "Sometimes it just feels that bloody way."

It's Saturday afternoon, Sunderland kicking off at 3 30pm in the second leg of the crucial match with Lincoln, the No 1 bus little burdened by passengers. The day's overcast, the sun making a momentary appearance before repenting of its temerity, the sheep (for the time being) safely and silently grazing.

Stanley seems quiet, too. Maybe most are indoors watching the big match on television, the red-and-whites for reasons of supporting evermore and the black-and-whites anticipating another outbreak of schadenfreude, as in these partisan parts is the custom.

St Thomas's church still shows no sign of imminent reopening. Next to it, the old vicarage has become Billy Hill House though not, at a guess, in acknowledgment of the bookmaker whose potential largesse could have made its purchase possible.

Near the forlorn football ground, new housing is called Wooley Meadows – probably more likely to sell than Black Road, formerly nearby – leading to St Thomas Court and Tanners Mews. Tanners Hall was once a copse nearby. A parked van promotes Creature Cuisine, presumably what once was known as dog food.

The village hall, reopened with the easing of restrictions on May 17, is unoccupied. The previous day, says its Facebook page, someone at the hall had been offering great boxes of what Sharon calls Haribo-type sweeties for £5 a pop – a regular treat, apparently.

"Check the kids' teeth," says Sharon, as I head off for the No 1, but with little inclination to go dental.

It's 5 30pm when I walk into Billy Row Club for the first time in 30-odd years. The last occasion had been a Stanley United players' reunion at which the principal guest was to have been Tommy Cummings, a centre half from Hetton-le-Hole who spent a season at Stanley before a long and successful career at Burnley, winning England B honours.

None back then had a mobile phone, no one had invented GPS. It didn't really explain why Tommy was two hours late, having been on the Hill Top for nine months but still – like many before and doubtless since – pitched up in the "wrong" Stanley.

The club's been closed throughout lockdown, only re-opening the day previously. Six or seven men and a couple of dogs are gathered, a greyhound wrapped snugly in a sort of canine top coat but still looking pretty fed up. Even the dogs around here remember the adage about ne'er casting a clout.

The match has just finished on the television, Sunderland beaten on aggregate. "I've never stopped crying," says one of the Newcastle fans, helplessly laughing. Another slyly supposes that it's all down to advanced social distancing, the need to keep Newcastle and Sunderland two leagues apart.

Though there are lads here who may suppose schadenfreude to be one of those faux Pilsner lagers, made somewhere tropical like Tow Law, they're still awfully good at it.

Until the turn of the 20th century, Billy Row Club was part of the Union – the Club and Institute Union – and run by a committee. A certificate on the wall suggests that it opened in 1872. Back in the day, they reckon, you couldn't get in on a Saturday night unless your name was on the back of the seat (though exceptions might be made for those willing to sing *Penny Arcade*.)

It was purchased privately, again came close to closure, and was bought by Trevor Smith five or six ("maybe seven") years ago. He's 61, an electrician, lives down the bank in Billy Row.

"My partner detests the place, hates it with a passion," he says. "All she says is get rid of it, get rid of it, but so long as I can cover the bills I'm not. It would have closed otherwise and it's the only place left for the old lads to go to for a drink. The average age is probably 65. There's nothing else for them, we're just all friends."

"Aye, and mickey takers" – he uses a slightly different phrase – "as well," says Dan Kerridge, his manager.

Trevor installed a dance floor, booked bands on Fridays and Saturdays, dancing on Sundays - a practice of which the Primitive Methodists, remembered in the previous chapter, would scarcely have approved – and joined a darts league. "That's what did my back," says Dan. "Carrying this lot around."

Tuesday was grab-a-granny night. "Real good grab-a-granny night," says Graham Hutchinson, also gathered around the table.

None of it worked. Now it's pretty much a drinking club, only open Friday to Sunday, using just one room. In the absence of what might be termed professional entertainment they now wait for the snow, stand by the window with their pint and watch the cars sliding one into another. "None of them has the wit to use the grit bin. It's the best show on earth," says Trevor.

Trevor blames the county council for withdrawing subsidy for late evening buses and successive governments for their unsympathetic attitude to the hospitality industry. "It's the same old thing, pubs and clubs are dying fast and no one's doing anything to stop it.

"When Gordon Brown allowed the supermarkets to sell beer, that was it. People could just go to the supermarket, buy what they wanted, stagger around the town and go home."

Though Trevor could never bring himself to vote Conservative – "not after what Thatcher did to the working man" – the truly extraordinary thing is that, in a former workmen's club in a former colliery community in the west of Co Durham, he's considerably outnumbered.

They're good lads, accepting and informed, and they criticise in detail both the policies of Durham County Council and of Laura Pidcock, the left-listing former Labour MP for NW Durham. Like Humpty Dumpty, she fell off the Wall. Since December 2019 the local MP has been Richard Holden, a Conservative and Dean Walker, among the Saturday afternoon crowd, is a card carrying Tory.

"There's a lot of Tories round here now. We'd rather roast our testicles over open flames than vote Labour again," he says, perhaps grateful that Stanley no longer gets much concessionary coal. "The biggest betrayal we've ever seen in this country is Labour and the working man. This is now like a Conservative Club. Who'd ever have thought that there'd be a Conservative Club in Billy Row?"

Dean warms appropriately to his theme. "He hasn't tekken his medicine yet," someone says.

Off the wall - Laura Pidcock

31

The talk's also of vanished pubs. Stanley had the Heights of Alma, the Earl Derby, the Wooley New Inn – known inexplicably as the White City – and the Robin Hood, now the Foresters, a restaurant and guest house where we hope to get feet beneath a table before many more chapters have been written. Just down from the club was the Shepherds Arms, down from that Nicky's, from that the Royal George and, along the road at White Lea, the dear old Dun Cow, hung with a vast collection of chamber pots and known locally as the Cow Tail or as Dode's.

The club had those queues mentioned earlier – "real queues, miles long" says Trevor – and an even bigger turnout on the occasion of the annual trip. "There'd be buses half way down Billy Row bank and all along Stanley front street," Trevor recalls. "Redcar, usually, highlight of the year."

Few regulars now come from the newer, more expensive, houses on the Hill Top. "They're mortgaged up to the hilt, can't afford to go out," says Trevor. "They've come down to our level, skint." Many others are far-ranging bikers, as familiar with the Pyrenees as with Peases West, members of the Squashed Frogs – true, no amphibian.

Today's one of the biker's birthdays, Trevor's got extra vodka in. Since the birthday boy can't stand football, they've all bought him a ball.

What, one apiece? "Oh aye," says Trevor. "I don't like bananas so they all bought me bananas when it was mine."

The bus back leaves just before 7pm, the birthday biker hasn't yet arrived. "When he does," says Trevor, "I think we might have a good drink tonight." And a toast to Lincoln City, an' all.

5: bench marks

May 25 2021

Long centuries of history notwithstanding, Barnard Castle has been propelled firmly onto the present-day map by the egregious Mr Dominic Cummings.

"He pitched up just down there, it was my mate who recognised him," says David Armstrong, pointing from his conservatory across the back garden and towards the turbulent Tees.

There's a wooden bench round the corner, bottom of the bank. Could it be the same unparliamentary seat on which the PM's former chief adviser tested his vision, found it functional but discovered that much of the rest of Britain couldn't believe his eyes? "Very likely," says David.

Traditionalists would in any case argue that his bungalow on the south bank of the Tees isn't in Barnard Castle at all but in the separate parish of Startforth, not even in Co Durham but in the North Riding of Yorkshire. It was, at least, until the Local Government Act of 1974, simpler days when the river provided a county line 85 miles long.

Unless his optics were illusory indeed, Cummings and party would have had to cross the 14th century County Bridge, which long marked the Durham/North Yorkshire border and where in the 18th century a gentleman called Cuthbert Hilton would conduct bogus but in-demand "marriage" ceremonies, besom buddies obliged to jump over a broomstick held across the county boundary to signal their illicit union.

Many such alliances were said to have ended disastrously – and co-habiting out of wedlock became known as living over the brush. Clever Mr Cummings probably knew that already.

Monsoon season, the rain stots staccato from David's conservatory roof, so loudly that - socially distanced by six feet – we've to raise voices to make ourselves heard. Alongside the road by the river there's a sign warning to beware of, or at least to be aware of, ducks. They alone will affectionately recall the maudlin month of May, 2021.

He's 85, a retired Co Durham head teacher and another of the Stanley Armstrongs. Like Hilary, his ennobled cousin, he also remembers Saturday evenings at Uncle Dick's, waiting for the sports papers, that hot metal miracle, to be thrown from a hurried van. "There were two, probably Pink and Green. I really just enjoyed listening to the fellers, waiting for the paper and then going home to watch the Billy Cotton Band Show."

Other shops, including Aunty Ethel's, seemed equally busy. "I remember once reading that Stanley had 27 shops, including fish shops and things. I can almost believe it," he says.

On Sunday mornings, sometimes in the evening as well, he'd walk – walk! – up Billy Row bank with his father and sister for services at Mount Pleasant (Primitive) Methodist chapel in Stanley.

Though born in Crook and later resident in Billy Row he gradually went up in the world, reaching the Hill Top upon marriage, and National Service discharge, in 1960. They lived in Cooperative Terrace. "We bought it for £900 and five years later sold it for £1,200," he recalls.

"We mightn't have been as poor as some people up there but just because I was a teacher, we certainly didn't think of ourselves as posh. You really didn't think about poverty, that's just the way it was. I'd been to grammar school, to university and had two years in the sergeants' mess but I don't think I was prepared for Stanley."

Drinking wasn't really a problem, he suspects, save on pay day when the White City stood between a Wooley collier's wife and his wits, and not necessarily in that order. Gambling was more of a concern, "There was an old quarry above Crook where every Sunday there was a big pitch and toss school. I think lots of money was won and lost."

Such illicit activity was also recalled in Allan Stobbs's 1989 book on the railways of south-west Durham, referenced in the next chapter. Allan, who lived in Crook back then, would take Sabbath walks up to the coke works spoil heaps at Roddymoor where, he recalls, sentries would be posted.

"The police must have known of this illegal activity but I can never recall a raid taking place. Perhaps the sentries were so effective that the police knew a raid would be futile."

The Armstrongs, of course, would be at worship. Family folklore cherishes the story of Jack and Lizzie, his grandparents, concluding one Sunday morning that they had just twopence ha'penny between them and wondering how much of it – widow's mite, near enough - to put into the chapel collection.

They'd opted for a ha'penny and were much gratified when, soon after their return from chapel, a neighbour called around with some freshly baked scones. "Mind," said Jack, "mebbe if we'd put a penny in, she'd have put some butter on, an' all."

David also tells the story of Red Alligator, the Bishop Auckland-trained winner of the 1968 Grand National, grazing – perhaps holidaying – at White Lea, near Stanley, shortly after his victory. "All that was holding him in was a single strand wire fence, I said to someone looking after him that he'd just jumped Becher's and The Chair and wasn't going to have much trouble with a little bit fence."

The chap looked unconcerned. "Divvent thoo worry, young un," he said. "He knaas when he's well off."

The whitewashed wall that helped enclose Stanley United's now sad old football ground? "The men got a load of bricks from Square House and built it themselves. In the middle was a little plaque expressing gratitude to J B Hood, who owned Square House.

"People were incensed, they didn't like J B Hood. By the following morning it had disappeared, chiselled out. You can still see where it was."

Inevitably, a genuflection to Samuel Johnson's celebrated dictum that when two Englishmen meet the first talk is of the weather, conversation again turns to what might be termed Stanley's extremes. As per forecast, it turns to the winter of 1947, and of 1963.

"In 1947 when we lived in Crook, there was a bus stuck outside St Thomas's church (Stanley) for weeks until some of the pitmen got shovels and dug it out. In 1963 we had a small front garden in Cooperative Terrace and didn't see it for months, that was when the snow was up to the tops of some of the houses. It was a wild, wild time but it helped prove we were a proper community."

Spread out on David's table are pictures of his Uncle Ernest with Sir Bobby Robson and the football World Cup – "I think that must have been the real World Cup," he says – and of Ernest, youthful but unmistakeable, in the Stanley cricket team.

They're all pretty much peas in a pod, the Armstrongs.

Another photograph shows a statue at York Cricket Club erected last year in memory of club captain Dan Woods, David's nephew, just 32 when he died from oesophagal cancer days before the first lockdown. Dan had been captain both of York and of Cheshire, colleagues and team mates raising £50,000 for the hospice which cared for him. David paid half the £3,000 cost of the statue. "We couldn't even have a proper funeral," he says.

The storm abating, talk turns from family tragedy and myopic mandarins to more memories of Stanley Hill Top.

David was born in Lax Terrace, not far from Crook Town's football ground. Both his parents had been teachers though his mother was obliged to resign – "you had to in those days" – when she married. Granddad Jack was a deputy at Wooley colliery and Sunday School superintendent at Mount Pleasant Methodist chapel, separated by about 400 yards of terraced street and long years of old habit from the Wesleyan Methodists of Wooley Terrace.

Co Durham's Methodists were a bit stand-offish like that. A few miles south on the A68, where Toft Hill and Etherley almost elide, the former Wesleyans and former Primitives maintained separate chapels, barely 100 yards apart, until the 1970s. Up at Forest-in-Teesdale, miles from pretty much anywhere, the two chapels almost faced one another, opposites not always attracting.

When finally Toft Hill said its last Amen, some members opted to attend the lovely little chapel at Wind Mill – two country miles away and perceived as Primitive – rather than the formerly Wesleyan Etherley chapel, literally around the corner.

Mount Pleasant, says David, was a "proper" Primitive Methodist chapel, no organ but a harmonium on the little stage, played sometimes by Mrs Roberts and sometimes by Aunty Ethel.

David's father, John, became headmaster of Billy Row school. At his cousin Jean's wedding to Stanley United captain Ronnie Tunstall, recalled earlier, David was the only escapee Crook fan to be, briefly, at the wedding breakfast.

He also remembers his Uncle Ernest's enthusiastic (shall we say) support for Stanley – "even when he was an MP he'd run up and down the pitch, alongside the linesmen, telling them where they were going wrong" – and the infamous FA Amateur Cup tie against Yorkshire Amateurs in 1948 when the bitterly cold conditions forced four home players permanently to seek sanctuary (if not, quite, salvation.)

Eye test - Dominic Cummings

Rules stipulated that, had Stanley been reduced to six men, the game would have had to be abandoned. "The committee were all urging them to come off. I've never been so ashamed in all my life" says David. "It was quite a nice day in Crook but when we got up the hill it was absolutely perishing, horrible. We had to go to Aunty Ethel's afterwards to dry out."

It wasn't always like that, of course. Though Stanley is best known for its views southwards, David recalls that on a good day, looking north-eastwards from the back gardens in Arthur Terrace, there were terrific views of Durham Cathedral.

For the Armstrongs, Methodism, Socialism and sport ran pretty much on parallel lines. Like his father, David was a long-serving local preacher though humbly doubting that he was as good. "My dad did things differently from me, preached at Waterhouses harvest festival 17 years running. I did it for two years then they decided they'd heard quite enough."

Like the workmen's club in the previous chapter, the two chapels also had eagerly anticipated annual trips – Whitley Bay usually, it's said. "For some folk Whitley Bay was like going abroad," says David. "They never got outside the county otherwise. The chapel trips were nothing like as big as the club trip, though."

Mount Pleasant chapel, long gone, was across the road from the village Institute, known thereabouts as the Tute, about which I've so far heard much, know little and am determined to learn more. Much the same applies to the specific location of Black Road and the Green Hut, which may leave little to colourful imagination but does little for location.

Both by road and by the path up the old mineral railway line,

two-and-a-half miles between Stanley and Waterhouses, are linked by Buttons Bank, an interesting exercise in where an apostrophe might legitimately take possession. A plaque on a bench alongside the railway path records that Alice and Thomas Button and their son Tommy worked Wooley Farm for 55 years. Buttons Place in Waterhouses dextrously sidesteps altogether the grammatical law of possession.

The Button family farm was also the northern extremity when Mount Pleasant's Methodists would lug their little harmonium, singing at every stop. On occasion there'd be a small orchestra, too. David recalls a similar Christmas carolling exercise at Billy Row chapel, when he asked for copies of the words and discovered they didn't need any because all they ever sang was *While Shepherds Watched*.

"There were about a dozen different tunes, including *Ilkley Moor Baht 'at*. We might have struggled with some of those, but we never forgot the words."

The internet also believes that the old line along Buttons Bank is used for 1k cycling time trials, records for both men's and women's events and probably not one of the pesky velocipedes fitted with a bell.

David was a Methodist local preacher for 41 years, led 1,878 services, wrote down every word of every sermon, familiar at both chapels in Tow Law, both in Billy Row, both in Stanley and the single chapel in Sunniside. All are now gone. In his last service, back in Barnard Castle shortly before his 70th birthday, he'd quoted verses from the Book of Deuteronomy about a land of wheat and barley and figs and olives and pomegranates and whatnot and vowed to have the same scripture read at his funeral.

National hero - Red Alligator

Translated, says David, it means "Divvent forget your browtins up."

He became a visionary head of Deerness Valley comprehensive school, west of Durham, a national executive member of the National Union of Teachers and secretary and treasurer of the constituency Labour Party. These days, five years a widower, he regrets that he's rather lost touch with folk.

Suffering like Dominic Cummings from eyesight problems, he also regrets that cataracts have prevented a recent return to his roots. "I really must try to get up to Stanley this summer. It's not that I don't love the place any more; I really, honestly do."

Similar feelings may not be attributed to the bloke on the Barney bench. The following day, the capricious Cummings tells a House of Commons select committee that he wishes he'd never heard of Barnard Castle and will never go near it again.

6: making tracks

June 12 2021

Hope Street in Liverpool has two cathedrals. Hope Street, Crook, has five pubs, three betting shops, two or three barbers, a nail bar, a tattoo parlour and a Greggs. It's 9 30 on a sun-blessed Saturday morning and already they're queuing outside Greggs.

Hope Street was also the location of Crook railway station, closed to passengers in 1964 and with a dozen or more lines radiating a couple of hundred yards northwards to Bankfoot Coke Works, founded by Pease and Partners in 1850 and covering 150 acrid acres.

"Bankfoot was Crook and Crook was Bankfoot," says Allan Stobbs in his 1989 book on the railways of south-west Durham, and no matter that some still called it Peases West. Some even inserted an apostrophe, but let's not (yet) get into bother over those pesky little blighters.

Tarred - Bank Foot cokeworks

In 1900, it's reckoned, around 2,000 men toiled at Bankfoot, the immediate site embracing Roddymoor pit and the by-product plants. Across the road, the Farrers Arms would open at 6am, 2pm and 10pm so that the poor workers might seek rehydration at the end of a thirsty shift. It now opens more sporadically.

The coke which in vast quantities was produced – around 200,000 tons a year, much of it from the 135,000 tons of coal extracted annually from Wooley Colliery at its post-war peak – is said by Michael Manuel to have been the best in the world, by Allan Stobbs the finest in the country and more modestly on the Durham Mining Museum's wondrous website to have been "well known."

Michael Manuel is Crook's meticulous and near-omniscient historian and was for many years one of the town's barbers. For Michael, it may not be necessary to explain, anything whatever from Crook and district has the bettering of the rest of creation put together. If Crook made corn plasters, they'd be the world's best, too.

Bankfoot by-products included tar – world class tar – benzole, creosote and sulphate of ammonia. There was also a brickworks. The men worked in clogs and in coats known as slops, records Michael – danger and death constant by-products, too.

The Durham Mining Museum chronicles seven fatalities, acknowledging that the lugubrious list is almost certainly incomplete. It includes three 16-year-olds – a greaser, a dauber and a brickmaker – and a 62-year-old cart man, killed after his horse took fright at the sound of a locomotive's whistle.

Recalling the death of one of the 16-year-olds in 1912, Michael's chronicle also notes that Edward Reed, a foreman bricklayer, and 16-year-old grease maker Robert Morris died in a rescue attempt. Two others were nominated for bravery awards.

Stobbs suggests potential, if improbable, benefits – the area's youngsters required to stand in the vicinity of the tar plant in the belief that the pungent fumes emanating from it were just the job – if not necessarily what the doctor ordered – for the whooping cough.

Medics might mock, but when last did a kid from Crook go through such fearful hoops? Things go better with coke.

After 115 years, the works closed in 1965, five million tons of heaped shale eventually and impressively cleared from the site. The pits were going, too. The Crook area alone had had 26. Soon they'd be sunk without trace.

Among many lines wheezing bronchitically from Bankfoot was the Stanley Incline, downhill all the way from Waterhouses and Wooley, worked on what clever folk call a self-acting principle – full wagons down, empties automatically back up – by a stationary engine housed at Mount Pleasant, on Stanley's eastern extremity.

For "stationary engine" read "search engine" and that throws up a little problem. Key "Stanley engine" and "Stanley Crook" into Google and results range from "car repairs near Crook" to *Stanley's Fire Engine*, a book for five-to-seven year-olds which doubtless is charming but which may not wholly be relevant.

To add to the frustration, there was another winding engine at West Stanley – that blooming big brother again – and that's the one which turns up. The *real* Stanley Engine, at any rate, was finally wound up in 1952. Save for a few photographs, nothing remains of it.

Barely 200 yards from the top of Hope Street, the eight-and-a-half mile Deerness Valley Way heads breathtakingly northwards up Stanley Incline, almost immediately past the Peases West sports centre where the weekend athletes are just getting under orders.

The plan's to walk up to Stanley, on through Waterhouses to Esh Winning and with an ulterior motive at the turning point. Field's in Esh Winning is one of only two coal-fired fish and chip shops remaining in North-East England – the other's at Beamish Museum, formerly frying in Hartlepool, where the

Nesting place - Christopher Wren

smokily aromatic offerings come wrapped in facsimile copies of the *Durham Advertiser*. Carrot and stick, the hope's for an early lunch.

"Are you ready?" asks the athletics coach of his charges. As ready as I'll ever be, guv, I murmur from the non-com side of the fence.

Such the prowess at the regeneration game, such the rural transformation, it's almost impossible to imagine the life limiting horrors, the great pungent Pease pudding, which daily enshrouded this site. Nor is imagination helped by an almost total absence of information boards.

Just one is evident, half-hidden near the Farrers, recording that Bankfoot had "at least" 18 by-products. Such the coke works reputation, so numerous the students from Germany and else-

Frying high - Fields' fish and chip shop

where, that in 1910 they built what became the Uplands Hotel – first owner Mr Schwartz – in order to accommodate them all. The war put a stop to all that, of course.

On a lamp post a bit further up, a planning application dated March 2021 seeks permission for 29 "affordable" apartments – what makes an apartment affordable? – and two "community workshops" on land above the sports centre. It's much to be hoped that it's been rejected.

Save for a few dormant sleepers, nothing suggests the site's hacky-black heritage though it might – in fairness – take an information board half the circumference of Peases West running track to tell the story of Bankfoot.

There are, however, an abundance of Durham County Council signs advising that it's a shared use route – walkers, cyclists, those on horseback – and urging folk to respect and "be nice" to one another.

A surprising number are already afoot, many accompanied by their dogs. Others go walkies with their earphones in as now is the way, artlessly sharing the music of the moment. *Oh what a beautiful morning* would be altogether more appropriate.

An amputee dog hirples past, quite remarkably, on all-threes. A canny cat, mouser if not Scouser, walks alone.

The Victorians thought the Stanley Incline "fearsome", the Deerness Valley Walk website merely supposes the gradient to be "moderate". It recalls another North-East use of the term, in response to well meant health enquiries. "Only moderate" is a euphemism, usually meaning that there'll be an empty bed in the morning and in that regard conveying much the same meaning as "fairly comfortable" or, worse, "as well as can be expected."

The climb's unrelenting, respite offered half way up by a bench in memory of Michael "Mick" Corner, 1961-2015. Somewhere around here – even here, even then – a pedestrian had been killed in 1876 when the wagonway train hit an "animal obstruction", the train split and the poor chap was in the wrong place.

Underground movement - Stanley Drift 1911

At the top, near where the Stanley Engine must have gone nowhere fast, a more elaborate and football themed wrought iron bench is dedicated to Wayne Clark – "Clarky", it says – a much loved son and brother and "awesome" mate, just 19 when he died in 2007.

A plaque invites Wayfarers to rest awhile and think, further

Levelling up – Stanley incline

bidding unnecessary. Stanley may not yet be the Promised Land – as opposed to the Wide World identified in the opening chapter – but it's still very good to be here, and (as another hymn writer puts it) to ponder anew.

It's also somewhere around here that locals are said to have been able to hear the miners chatting as they headed to work underground – suggesting that while their hearing was remarkable it still wasn't as vivid as their imagination – and where men of Cromwell's army are reputed to have made camp en route to the Battle of Worcester, the last encounter of the English Civil War, in 1651.

Certainly it's true that many had been raised around Tyneside by Major General Harrison – and unlike many Newcastle sides of more recent times, they were victorious. Poor Charles II had ordered £343 3s worth of uniforms from the Worcestershire Clothing Company and, tail between his legs, never paid. More than 350 years later, in 2009, his namesake the Prince of Wales finally coughed up – though not the £47,000 interest which by that time was said to have accrued.

Further folklore suggests that the nearby Wren's Farm is so named because the great architect Sir Christopher Wren took his holidays in Stanley when not designing cathedrals and things. That one may be a little more difficult to substantiate.

The Deerness Valley Walk, officially part of the W2W – the Walney to Wearside cycle way – is as floral as it is fragrant, as sylvan as it is golden and, yes, as verdant as it is vertiginous. Little subsidiary paths wander off, coquettishly, in all directions, adventure for another day.

Those more naturally inclined, and less optically encumbered,

Flying high - Wooley men and their banner

talk of broad oaks and handsome hazels, of red campion and dogs mercury, wild garlic, bluebells and stichwort. A previous walking companion had tried to explain the meteorological runes that might be read from frog spawn alongside the path into Waterhouses, though with what might best be deemed limited success.

The only problem is the cyclists, to whom niceness is municipally encouraged but not always warranted. Isn't it still the law that bikes must be fitted with a bell, or at least what they call an audible warning device? Where's the Serious Crime Squad when you need them?

The worst of them simply steal up, hugger-mugger, from the rear. Others announce their imminence pantomime-style –

Collier lads – Wooley miners in 1890

"Behind you" – all very well save for those of what the BBC used to call a nervous disposition.

The pedestrians, conversely, are almost unfailingly friendly. A dog walker stops to report that, the previous day, he'd paid £12 at Aldi for 24 cans of 5.8 per cent strength lager – mostly, he says, to help him through England's televised European Championship football match against Croatia the following afternoon. Mind, he adds temperately, he hopes it'll tide him over the rest of the weekend, an' all.

Half way between Stanley and Waterhouses is that bench dedicated to Alice and Thomas Martin Button and their son Thomas – the Buttonses as thereabouts they are remembered – who'd farmed the area for 55 years and who, it may be recalled from an earlier chapter, constituted the northern extreme of the Primitive Methodists' annual travels with a harmonium.

In Waterhouses, where the little church was built with bricks hauled up from Bankfoot, another bench remembers Frank Roberts (1911-98) – "a son of the Deerness Valley."

Though the Deerness Valley railway from Durham shuffled as far as Waterhouses Colliery, Waterhouses passenger station was in Esh Winning. A sort of good English compromise, Esh Winning football club has its splendidly scenic ground in Waterhouses.

The line closed to passengers in 1951, save for the annual exodus to Durham Big Meeting and the workmen's club trip to the briny. Goods traffic ceased in 1964. The trackbed heads eastwards from Waterhouses to Esh Winning and to the Elysian promise of a coal-fired lunch.

Five generations of the Field family have been frying tonight, or at least most nights, since 1915. For the centenary they turned out not just the Worshipful Mayor of Durham but the village brass band, an' all.

The first shop, and the second, were in Cornsay Colliery, a couple of miles away. Family legend has it that "Old Bob" Field, down on his luck in the 1920s, was walking to Witton Park – near Bishop Auckland – in search of work when he bumped (as you do) into a bookie's runner and invested his last £2 on a horse called Light Dragoon. Unburdened, it won at 100-1.

Thus enriched, Old Bob sold the Cornsay business, opened new premises in Esh Winning front street and the village garage business, too.

These days Esh Winning has two chip shops – as, indeed, had the Hill Top – the other called Market Plaice, debate continuing long into Deerness Valley winter nights over which is the better. There are two Chinese takeaways and a pizza joint, too.

At Field's there's just one problem: the modern day need to wear a face mask indoors, producing both condensation and consternation, means that I am wholly unable to offer an interior description of the premises save (for some reason) that it sells black pudding and cheesy chips, not necessarily together. It may also be reported that it might soon have a second claim to quaintness, if not quite antiquity. In these increasingly cardsharp days they insist upon cash only, and not even IOUs from Shildon lads with honest faces.

Shildon lads? The head fryer asks if I'm from South Shields, explaining that there's been a telephone call from a coach party of Shields lads hungrily headed their way, the workmen's club trip in reverse. The temptation to ask if I look like a Sand Dancer, or indeed a coach party, is happily resisted. I head for a bench up the sunlit street and enjoy a £6 lunch before setting off back for Stanley.

Doubtless it is a sign of advancing years that downhill sections seem to be levelling up, as Boris would put it, and that the ascents appear ever steeper. The return leg calls for a breather on Buttonses' bench – the apostrophe must by now be supposed functional, if not defensible. Where's the White City when you need it?

Where the railway path meets the road from Stanley to Waterhouses, there's something rather strange. Five slices of white bread have carefully been arranged by the roadside in quintessential formation akin to the Olympic rings.

If it is indeed Olympian, it seems an awfully long way from Tokyo. If it's biblical, what happened to the two fishes and if it's the work of some hitherto unsuspected Stanley secret society then no one's letting on. Besides, isn't it Tow Law which has all the hugger-mugger Masons?

After a quick detour through Grahamsley, it's a little more than ten miles and a little before two o'clock when I collapse into the Farrers – disarmed these days, restyled "pub and restaurant" – in search like the Bankfoot coke men of refreshment at the end of a perspiring shift.

The No 1 again awaits. In Hope Street, there's still a queue outside Greggs.

7: housey housey

June 21 2021:

There's a story which I tell the Women's Institutes and their ilk about the time, early 1970s, when I was invited to open the village carnival at Mickleton, in Teesdale.

The chairman by way of introduction said how pleased they were to welcome Mike Amos but admitted that I hadn't been the first choice – the first choice was Mike Neville, a hugely popular presenter of regional television news. "Mike Neville was £50," the chairman added. "Mike Amos was nowt."

This afternoon's bingo session at Stanley Village Hall is a bit like that.

Plan A was to spend a day at the village school, tentatively and enthusiastically agreed with David Christie, the head, but subject to Boris's road map getting somewhere by June 21. It hasn't.

Plan B was to catch up with the locally omniscient Dave Ayre, with his wife at the care home in Billy Row, but that's also scuppered by Covid caution. Residents are still just allowed five named visitors. "Sorry," says the lady on the phone, "you aren't on the list."

The weekly bingo was further down the agenda, though village hall secretary/treasurer Valerie Singleton is happy to agree a card marking appearance.

"Valerie Singleton? Why does that name ring a bell?"

"Blue Peter" she says.

"Oh aye."

Valerie was born and raised on the Hill Top, now lives down the hill in Crook but is a (very) frequent traveller on the No 1 bus. "I was the fifth child, a bit crowded in a two-up two-down so they offered us a new house in Crook, inside toilet, everything. We still had family in Stanley, though, always came back up."

She still belongs Stanley, she adds, as North-East folk do. It's a most appealing use of the word.

It's a pretty bleak Midsummer Day – cold, overcast and with rain in the air. The unworthy thought occurs that if this is Stanley on Midsummer's Day, what's it like on Midwinter's Night.

Though it's lunchtime when I shiver past the school, the playground's silent and deserted. Either they're still eating their dinners – about which the head has greatly enthused – or they're being kept indoors for reasons of common humanity.

A few hundred yards further on, at the junction with the road to Waterhouses, rests another ornately crafted memorial bench, this one in wood, chiefly featuring two recumbent dogs. At the base is the inscription "On a warm summer evening on a train bound for nowhere." There's no evident identity: Dave Ayre would know.

Across the fields comes the sound of happily playing children, weather-proofed like a commercial for suet dumplings: they've had their dinners, anyway.

Though a house in Arthur Terrace is garlanded with balloons and birthday bunting, none – so far as infirm eyes may tell – flies the flag for England in the imminent European football championship. They do in B**** R**.

Past the forlorn football ground and towards the village hall, I wander down what once was Jobson Terrace but appears vividly to have been re-imagined as Jobson Meadows. Where once 500 folk might have lived cheek-by-jowl, now stand five handsome houses. It's positively posh: for Jobson Meadows, read Millionaires' Row.

Note to self: come back and try to talk to the residents: the chapter can be called Jobson's choice.

This one can be called Housey Housey.

An early memory of growing up in Shildon is from about 1961 when they proposed to close the Hippodrome cinema, the last of four in a town of 12,000 people, and turn it into a bingo hall.

Led by Paul Elwell, an Albert Street contemporary whose dad owned a toy shop and who had a smashing model railway, a "Ban the bingo" protest was launched with a nod to the Campaign for Nuclear Disarmament then gathering pace and, sadly, with as little success. It got on the telly, though.

My mam was secretly delighted by defeat. She was a bingo addict – semi-professional, you might say – and though well accustomed to returning empty handed, by no means a good

Benchmarks - memorial to Christian Michael Carswell

loser. We played at home, too, twopence a line and sixpence a house, but in the intervening 60 years I've hardly had eyes down at all. Clearly there has been a genetic hiccup.

Just seven others are gathered in the village hall, they and Valerie who's the caller. All are female, all getting on a bit, all greatly welcoming. About half are still in Stanley, half – though not 3.5 – exiled to Crook. "Mind," warns Valerie, "they're cheeky fond, this lot."

"It's freezing out," says Heather Moore whose father-in-law Tommy Moore and husband Alan, now 71, started the village

Memorial to Wayne Clark

taxi business from their home – and later the former Miners' Institute – in `1968. It's now run by Alan's sons Stephen and Colin.

"It's healthy," insists Marie Irvine. "I was never bad until I moved to Crook." Few take off their outdoor jackets, nonetheless.

Once there might have been twice as many, numbers depleted by age, infirmity and by the inexorable alternative. Former players are recalled: "Mrs Mason, Hilda, Audrey, Mavis, her down the road, Lilian…." Once, just once, they had a feller. "You know" they say, "Spot."

The Monday afternoon session costs £2, another £1 for the raffle and another for the snowball, a sort of accumulator which has to be won on 55 or fewer of the ninety possible numbers and for which it's necessary to have been playing for four weeks to be allowed in with a shout. The prize pot's grown – snowballed – to £92. "No one's won it for a canny while," says Valerie.

"We haven't been here for a canny while," they chorus.

Prize money's £1 50 for a line, £2 50 full house. "You can win a house and go home out of pocket" says Valerie.

Each book has six tickets, simultaneously scrutinised and marked off with something called a dabber. They offer to lend me one but, not being much of a lad for technology, I persuade them that felt tipped pen will suffice. They had in any case warned against banging the table with the thing. "Bang the table and you get put out," someone says.

Save for "top of the shop" and an occasional dander down Downing Street – you know, number 10 – Valerie bothers little with bingo lingo, or at least its more arcane excesses. I'm thrown not just by the sixfold unfamiliarity of it all but by the need simultaneously and almost ambidextrously to translate thoughts into notes, which you can't really do with a dabber.

The indelible local legend of Stanley United v Yorkshire Amateurs again comes to mind, not least for a bingo beginner long domiciled in the North Riding, but that's one for a later chapter. The outcome's much the same, mind.

Another semi-legible note recalls Edward Thompson's, a Sunderland printing firm founded in 1867 and with no great mark in history until 1958 when – three years before Britain's first bingo hall - they produced their first ticket. By 1965 they were turning out 50 million each week.

Back home, the company website suggests that bingo is yet luckier for some, even if a PhD seems necessary in order to take part. "We supply all the major players," says the website which may or may not embrace the lovely ladies in Stanley village hall.

The website also has details of QT electronic bingo tablets, of jackpot feature systems and not just of dabbers but – get this – of digi-dot double ended dabbers. Between the lines, Fred Flintstone comes to mind – a reference which may in itself be arcane but I make a quick note of that one, an' all.

A little out of sequence, but Edward Thompson's announced in February 2022 that it was to close, with the loss of 53 jobs. "Covid completely changed the market" said Paddy Cronin, the chief executive. "We were built on a bet, but our luck ran out."

The village hall regulars are much more versatile, of course,

more comfortable with multi-tasking. Someone tells between numbers of a cousin up in Waterhouses whose long passage has been requisitioned by a film company which wants to shoot a chap wearing a rucksack swiftly turning round and breaking a picture of ducks. Something like that, anyway.

The conversation turns to other films made thereabouts – Inspector George Gently quite a regular, Ripping Yarns once filming a bank robbery episode in Tow Law, and no matter that there was no longer a bank. Hadn't someone once seen Catherine Zeta Jones out among the wind turbines?

"It's a very funny thing," says someone else, not entirely relevantly, "that though I've never eaten a Twix bar in my life, I can't stand them."

In the second of five games, I win a thirty shilling line. In the next I call on house – dab hand, or what? – the ticket duly scrutinised. "If you come back next week, we're putting someone on the door," says one of the ladies, affably, declining the offer to donate the sudden windfall to hall funds.

"I never win nothing," someone else says, the temptation to deliver a third form lecture on use of the double negative deflected by the need, however metaphorical, to keep a great many balls in the air.

At the interval I win a big bar of Aero in the raffle. Money goes to money, they say, though there are no further successes and the jackpot simply snowballs. Lucky for some, nonetheless.

Formerly known as the Social Centre, the spacious village hall is on the site of the Green Hut mentioned earlier, the land given by the National Coal Board. The replacement building, completed at a cost of £47,000 in 1988, was funded by donations from the Banks opencast mining group and from Persimmon, who'd built many of the new homes. Valerie's been secretary/ treasurer for 22 years.

"The village men would come home from work, have their tea and then come round here to help out, digging foundations and all sorts," says Valerie. "You don't see that today."

Though it's an excellent facility, Covid has claimed the weekly pilates, yoga and taekwondo sessions. The toddler group is expected to return in September while the radio hamateurs will continue to transmit on Thursday evenings and with whom I must take the air. Financially, says Valerie, they're still sound.

"It's down to good housekeeping. We used to collect membership fees but there were so few it wasn't worth it. The newcomers aren't interested in the community in the same way. I'm sure they're very nice people but they only come here when they want something, like a children's party so they make a mess here and not in their own homes."

Numbers up, they're quick to leave, though some will be meeting for coffee the following morning. While waiting for the bus, they try to recall the businesses which traded along the front street when Stanley, and England, really was a nation of shopkeepers. There was Tow Law Co-op, another Co-op, Walter Willson's, two fish shops, Smith's the bookie's, Albert Simpson the draper, an ironmonger, Armstrong's paper shop, a butcher, a baker and (who knows) maybe the grease monkeys as well. A GP would hold surgeries next to Holmes's, down the bottom end.

"The post office was the last to go," says Marie, "a little general dealer's in the end. All gone now."

June Taylor – "I was a Liddle, there's still a lot of Liddles in the village" – was born in Francis Street, moved to one of the 102 houses in Wooley Terrace, attended Wolsingham Grammar School ("one of about six from the village") lived in Tow Law when her husband found work there but hastened home to Stanley. "It's my resting place," she says, unequivocally. "It was just like coming home; people are so kind here.

"It doesn't really matter about not having a shop. You can get the bus down to Crook, do your shopping, meet folk – half of them are from Stanley, anyway – and come home again. Personally I can't wait to get back."

I'm on the bus with them, though carrying on to Darlington and – since there are no shops in Stanley – with a large Aero bar for a rather belated lunch.

Nearly a month after the lucky-for-some bingo, July 17, we're headed down the A68 after a sun blessed week in the Scottish borders and detour the couple of miles eastwards to Stanley. It's the most beautiful summer day. "I wonder when it was last 28 degrees in Stanley?" says Sharon, by which she means 28 degrees Celsius and not Fahrenheit, familiar in former times.

Partly I want to check if there's any sign of St Thomas's church reopening for Sunday worship – there isn't – partly to see what Sharon makes of that vividly poignant bench, a warm summer evening on a train bound for nowhere, alongside the road to Waterhouses. At once the words strike a chord, or possibly a guitar string.

A little googling reveals that it's the opening line of The Gambler, a No 1 hit for gravel-voiced American country singer

Kenny Rogers, aged 81 when he died in 2020. The chorus may also be familiar:

You've got to know when to hold 'em

Know when to fold 'em,

Know when to walk away

And know when to run....

Thus ignited, further research clarifies that the bench is a memorial to Christian Michael Carswell, Chrissy to his friends, found hanged at his home in Howden-le-Wear, near Crook, in 2013. He was just 16, 6ft 6ins tall, had attended Stanley village school and formerly lived within sight of where the bench now mourns his too-brief years. The Gambler was played at his funeral.

His grieving dad had posted on the message board of If U Care Share, a charity which addresses suicide among young men. "We will never be the people that we were before that day," he wrote. "Christian was larger than life, but God had other plans for him. We miss him terribly."

Family and friends had raised £2,000 for the bench, carved by Tommy Craggs and depicting Christian's dogs, Raggy and Stella, and his motor bike helmet and gloves. Lauren, his sister, had talked to *The Northern Echo* in 2014, describing him as a big friendly giant.

"It's a bench about him, but we also hope that anyone thinking of killing themselves will come and see it, It may change their view. It's about all that my brother was, as well as what he might have been. He was very popular and everyone knew him.

He was very funny and a good listener, like a counsellor to a lot of his friends. Losing him was just terrible, so awful."

A previous chapter noted another bench, dissimilar in style but similar in purpose, atop Stanley Incline. Made by Graham Hopper, a celebrated metal sculptor based down the bank in Willington, it was a tribute to Wayne Clark, from Crook, aged 19 when found dead at his home in November 2006.

Clarky was football mad, it was said, though the bench represents every element of his life. Like Christian Carswell's, barely half a mile away, it was subscribed by family and friends as a means of remembrance and of reflection.

Christian's bench had had a plaque, headed "The Thinking Seat", and with lines to make you weep. "If love could have saved you, you would have lived for ever."

Later I learn of the death in similarly tragic circumstances of Dylan Lee, another local 19-year-old, his thronged funeral held at St Thomas's during lockdown. It's a truly dreadful trilogy.

In what's likely to be the book's lengthy gestation, we shall doubtless rest again at both those melancholy and tranquil places. The chapter dated November 19 will look much more closely at Dylan's terrible death. "You've got to know when to hold 'em, know when to fold 'em" will resonate for ever.

8: Jobson's choice

June 26 2021

Among the precious few reasons that Sharon keeps me, or those to which she will admit, is my ability to see off unwanted callers, particularly the pesky Jehovah's Witnesses.

In journalism such unsolicited intrusion is called doorstepping – some might suppose foot-in-the-doorstepping. These changing times it happens very little. You can't be digitally doorstepped, can you?

Truth to tell, I didn't do very many knocking stories, though there was the infamous evening when a few of us, winding down at length in the pub in Darlington after a hard day's mischief making in the newsroom, were disturbed both by a ferocious storm and by the sound of a great many emergency vehicles splashing past. There'd been some spectacular flash flooding, it transpired.

Together we stirred long-dormant thoughts of holding the front page and, in a state of what we imagined to be mere merriment, headed towards the apocalypse. I plodged up a garden path, the door answered by a sturdy chap with mop and bucket.

He took one appraising look, at once appreciative of the situation. "Come in," he said, "and sit down before you fall down."

Today's another wet one – what that Scottish chap on Tyne Tees Television used to call dreich – and again I'm required to doorstep, to explain in the five seconds between cautious opening and furious slamming that I'm not trying to sell anything, nor trying to convert them to anything – not even North Sea Gas – and not, definitely not, one of those scummers.

I'm back on Jobson Meadows – formerly Jobson Terrace, a long row of two-up two-down colliery houses with a tin bath in front of the fire and a netty, perhaps even a two-holer, at a sensible (if not wholly sanitary) distance at the bottom of the yard. The *Northern Despatch* in 1967 reported that only eight of the 40 houses in Jobson Terrace were inhabited and that even they were "semi-derelict."

Despite protests from many residents, some of whom had bought their houses from the Coal Board – for between £25-£60 *The Northern Echo* reckoned at the time – an estimated 240 houses were demolished in the early 1970s, most occupants moved down to Billy Row.

On the Jobson Terrace site, the transformation is impressive and extraordinary. Rightmove, the estate agency, puts the average Jobson Meadows house price at around £400,000, a comparative giveaway. There are parts of England where a detached garage would cost that.

Immediately across the road, a well-equipped and remarkably unvandalized children's playground is still identified by Durham County Council as Jobson Terrace. Another sign ordains that there is to be no smoking in the playground. Not even Woodbines, penny a tab.

Jobson Meadow has a number of smart houses but the five at the end in every sense stand out. Most have three storeys, the better to enjoy the view (if the mist ever lifts, of course.) One of that handsome quintet has seven bedrooms, five bathrooms and just three permanent occupants. "We have two dogs as well," says Dawn Craggs, though the pets' sleeping arrangements are unclear.

Another, barely smaller, is occupied by Lynn Davison and her husband Ian – she born and raised in Billy Row before spending 30 years in London. "I could never have imagined Stanley changing like this," she says.

Downsides? "The winter," she says, at once.

Barely 100 yards away, a one-bedroomed former aged miners' bungalow on High Road is on the market for £71,000 – "investment opportunity" – a two-bedroomed bungalow for £100,000. In St Thomas Court, a much more recent development, a semi-detached two-bedroomed house is £110,000 ("ideal for first home owner") and a detached house with three bedrooms ("spacious and modern") £145,000.

Elsewhere in the village, location not specified, a "barn conversion", embracing 4.4 acres, a separate cottage, three paddocks and a stable block is on the market for £600,000. "Ideal for equestrian interests," it says. Horses for courses, no doubt.

Nothing's listed for Mount Pleasant and Francis Street, the long and long-familiar main road through the village, though Rightmove reckons the average Mount Pleasant house price to be £41,500 – "down 59 per cent from the 2006 peak of £101,363."

Is that mathematically correct? Was there really a property boom in Mount Pleasant 15 years ago or do they just pull these figures out of cyberspace? What was that in the opening lines of the prologue about estate agents?

Building Jobson Meadows to overlook Mount Pleasant may on any argument be supposed going up in the world, and seems a bit like building Mayfair round the corner from Old Kent Road – and that's no offence whatever to Old Kent Road.

The knock's answered at all five houses at the business end of Jobson Meadows. Though all are civil, none invites me inside from a mizzly, drizzly, thoroughly miserable morning (and though it makes writing notes a bit more difficult, I don't for a moment blame them.) Besides, Dawn has dogs.

Rob O'Dell, married to Tracey and with eight-year-old twins Farrah and Savannah, says at once that the main attraction was the reputation of the village school – "small classes, excellent teachers" – though they also love the quiet, the fresh air and the absence of traffic.

He can't really comment on the community spirit, though. "We only moved in April 2020 and have pretty much been in lockdown ever since. The people in the street seem very nice, though."

Recreational use - play park and Jobson Meadows

Dawn, who lives with her partner Steve Parbsey and their son Darryl, grew up in Temperance Terrace – Grahamsley, strictly, is it not? – attended school in Peases West and Wolsingham before heading to London as a 17-year-old. "It took us two years to sell our house down there but they held this for us and we're really happy that they did.

"The quiet's the main thing, the quiet and the countryside. It's a beautiful house, we haven't a mortgage, we absolutely love it in Stanley."

Lynn, up from Billy Row, moved into their new home almost ten years ago. "It's really peaceful apart from the dog walkers – I don't have dogs. I don't think we'll be going anywhere else now."

Vaguely encouraged, I head back down to Co-operative Terrace for a little supernumerary doorstepping at Innisfree, an attempt to answer the question posed in the first chapter about whether that terraced house is named after the lake island in W B Yeats's poem and, if it is, why.

The chap's friendly enough but says that they've just moved there and he has no idea. "It used to be the post office," he adds, "maybe that'll help." If the rain continues like this, Stanley itself may turn into a lake island; even Bill and Ben across the road are looking a bit under the weather.

However dilatory its progress, for once the X1 bus can't come soon enough. Fair drookit, as they say in The Broons, I've even a bit of sympathy for the JWs.

9: union dues

July 21 2021

Covid's clutches further eased, temperature touching 80 degrees in old money, it's possible at last to sit with Dave Ayre under an umbrella outside the West Lodge Care Home in Billy Row, rated "good" in all areas by the Care Quality Commission and "lovely" by Dave and Doris.

He'll turn 90 on August 3, lived for all but the first year of his life on the hill top, became a militant trade union official – not just part of the union, but the beating heart of the union – gained two Open University degrees after leaving Stanley school at 13, helped write a book, rode a push bike well into his 80s and is a long serving churchwarden at St Thomas's, which isn't bad for an agnostic.

A what? "It was Doris," he explains. "Me mother was a big chapel goer, big Wesleyan, but Doris loved St Thomas's dearly so I thought that if I could do a bit, I would. When you love someone to bits and it's something they live for then you can get on with the bugger, too. I don't see why church people have to be devout."

They moved down to West Lodge last year. "I'm fine and she's better than I am," says Dave, sitting in stockinged feet in a wheelchair. "I never wanted to leave Stanley, always thought that Billy Row folk looked down their noses a bit, but we've come on a treat down here."

The church's regular congregation is still tiny, its future greatly uncertain. "I think," says Dave, "that we're not snooty enough for some."

He is the very best of men – principled, personable, a workers' champion, a people's champion, a veritable breath of fresh Ayre – but for the interviewer presents a slight dilemma. Though not what unlettered people call pitmatic – he never worked there – his language is decidedly rooted in Co Durham, accent seemingly broader with age. Should he be quoted in Queen's English, for ease, or in dialect for authenticity?

Durham wins. Since the spelling is the same, however, it should be explained that the word "father" is pronounced not as in "rather" but as in "gather", that "Billy Row" is pronounced as in "Silly Car" and that when Dave talks of going to Durham he means – like many more – Durham Big Meeting, the beloved Miners' Gala.

Readers from outside the county palatine must for the moment imagine for themselves what a netty might have been, and what a windy pick.

His assertion that Stanley was widely and derogatorily regarded as the "plate ends" is also slightly confusing, at least to us Shildon lads. At Timothy Hackworth Junior Mixed and Infants, the plate ends what you saved until last, the best bits of the school dinner. On the Hill Top, clearly, they had something else on their plates.

His parents moved from Crook to Stanley – Wooley Terrace, that straitened street of 102 houses with a cold tap apiece and a row of netties out the back –when his hitherto unemployed dad got a job at Wooley pit. At five Dave started at Stanley school, at five-and-a-bit wished never to see it again.

The only teacher he liked answered to Titchy Taylorson – "little feller," says Dave, perhaps unnecessarily. The two Misses

Williamson were vicious, he says, especially the younger one. Joe Brooks, the headmaster, never really liked him, either – "but mebbe he had a good right, I was probably a handful."

He also remembers watching German aircraft bombing the Co Durham coast, around Hartlepool. "You could follow them all the way doon, but one time one came inland – mebbe lost – and dropped a bomb about 100 yards off us. It left a big crater."

More conventional childhood memories include climbing up and down the piles of concessionary coal left outside the colliery houses and chasing along the netty roofs. "Growing up in Stanley was bloody fantastic. We were mebbe a bit wild, always getting wrong and aal the time playing in the woods. We knew the names of aal the trees and aal the birds. Mind, we'd nivver have hurt any of them. I don't think we were ever conscious of being poor. It's just the way life was."

They'd also "analyse" the homeward miners. "You could tell who'd been in the New Inn and who hadn't. I divvent knaa why they called it the White City, it was nivver very white to start with."

So why didn't he follow his dad down the shaft? "Me father took us doon one Friday night and for all the riches in the world, aa'd nivver gan doon again. With it being a Friday night there weren't many working and you could hear the props creaking and the machinery gannin'. They'd just got windy picks and me dad thowt they were wonderful, except that there was so much dust he couldn't see.

"It killed him, just 62, he couldn't breathe. When they did the post mortem, his lungs were just like two little lumps of coke. That was the pits for you; he didn't have a chance."

The Durham Mining Museum's wonderfully comprehensive website records that at its peak, shortly after World War Two, Wooley Colliery employed almost 700 men – all but 100 underground – and produced 135,000 tons of coal a year. It also lists 36 deaths in the century before the pit closed in 1963, many from falls of stone, mordantly adding that the list is by no means likely to be complete.

William Brooks was just 14 when on January 3 1883 he fell off a waggon and was "run over on the railway leading to Wooley Colliery"; James Mason had also been 14 when crushed by tubs 12 years earlier.

Thomas Pyrah died down Wooley pit in 1887 – "while following his employment he ruptured his bowels" – Thomas Haydon fatally ruptured a blood vessel while lifting a stone, Hilton Hughes was burned by gas, Luke Welsh decapitated by the descending cage while looking down the shaft. John Bell, a shifter, was 71 – "stumbled against a shear and cut his face." The pit got him in the end.

The list continues lugubriously. "You can see what I mean," says Dave, "can't you?"

Instead he became an apprentice bricklayer – "bottom of the pile" – at once joined the union and tried to enlist others. "I didn't do badly but one lad absolutely refused, wouldn't be on. I persisted and he gave me a good hiding, had to be pulled off by some other union lads. They tellt us to behave mesel'. I'm not sure that I did."

Conscripted into the Durham Light Infantry, he was posted with the British Army on the Rhine, excelled at cycling and cross country running and became batman to a major. "I never wanted to be owt more than a private, not even in the army," he says, poor bloody Infantryman and proud of it,

He'd carried on cycling into his 80s, sometimes in time trials. "I gave them up," says Dave. "It wasn't fair on the timekeeper, having to wait around for me to finish."

Frequently blacklisted for union activity, he became a long-serving secretary of the Crook branch of UCATT, the construction workers' union, a member of the extreme left wing Socialist Workers Party and was actively involved in other trade union activity. "I was never full-time, never wanted to be, but our

Stalwart - Dave Ayre

record of winning cases was phenomenal. Me father always supported it, told me to be sure to pay me union money and me rent money but in that order, said it was better to belong to a bad union than nee union at all."

Retired headmaster David Armstrong, featured in an earlier chapter, recalls an occasion during the 1983 miners strike when Dave had helped attract a substantial donation from a French chap and asked David along to ensure nothing was lost in the translation. "It was at the Cow Tail at White Lea," says David. "I think it was quite a good night."

Around Co Durham, of course, the SWP is usually only sighted at the Big Meeting, forlornly trying to flog newspapers with blood-red mastheads and calls to militancy. "It we sold six all day we thought it was a treat," he recalls. "We never convinced anyone that Socialism was the thing."

Having hated school, he also discovered education, completed all the union courses and then, 40-odd years ago, gained those two degrees with the newly launched Open University. "Social science, I loved it. It was just relaxed, informal learning, completely different from school. I discovered that I enjoyed writing, too. I never thought of it as lessons, the degrees were just a bonus."

Some encouraged him to try for a third degree – professor level, they insisted. "I didn't like the sound of it," says Dave. "Professors were gaffers. I nivver wanted to be a gaffer all my life."

It was back in 1995 that Granville Gibson, then the Archdeacon of Auckland – a sort of assistant bishop – blew into St Thomas's church at Stanley, told them it would have to close and was confronted by Ernie Stoker, long-serving organist and much else.

"Over my dead body it will," said Ernie, though respectfully enough, of course. "He took his cap off, put it under his arm and then tellt him," says Dave. "Ernie was always respectful."

The parish magazine merely recorded that Archdeacon Gibson had "incurred Ernie's wrath."

Faced with a discordant organist, perhaps remembering the venerable ecclesiastical adage that the difference between an organist and a terrorist is that it's easier to negotiate with a terrorist, the archdeacon said that if St Thomas's folk could prove within six months that the embers could be ignited, then he'd help them do it.

The archdeacon even discovered damage to stained glass windows – gales, inevitably – for which they'd forgotten to claim. Too busy fighting Category D, he said.

Eight years later, a service to dedicate three new windows was led by Michael Turnbull, the Bishop of Durham. One was in memory of Ernie Stoker, who had indeed died, another acknowledged Granville Gibson and the third saluted International Workers' Memorial Day, to which an earlier chapter alluded.

"A solemn warning to the corporate world of the consequences of capital being more important than people," it was said (though heaven alone knows by whom.) Dave Ayre was there, too, mufflered like a latter day Bob Cratchit, and looking awfully pleased.

Music ranged from Amazing Grace to the Trimdon Grange Explosion, in which the populace is urged not to think about tomorrow lest they disappointed be. "It really is a wonderful

occasion," said Bishop Michael, "quite marvellous what you have done."

So what now, what about tomorrow? Closed for regular worship since Mothering Sunday 2020, St Thomas's is known internally to be deteriorating. Dave – "it's completely against most people's idea of left wing politics, but I love being a church member" – hopes still to fight the good fight, even from West Lodge.

"The church was falling to bits and we put it back together both physically and in numbers. It's like a union branch, if there's only one person comes along to the meeting then it's worthwhile. It would be a terrible shame if it had to close, and I fear that it might, but you never know what's going to happen, do you?"

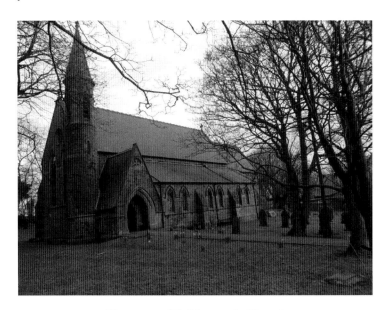

Threatened St Thomas's Church

He and Doris lived for many years on the Heights of Alma, views on a good day to Yorkshire and on a half-decent one to Toft Hill. The fire – "not bleezin', just smouldering a lot of the time" – was always in, all year round. "It was just nice to come back to, you felt you were home," says Dave, in whom the fire never wanes, either.

As with St Thomas's however, he fears a village in decline. "It was Category D. Once they knocked down Wooley Terrace, Jobson Terrace and Stanley Terrace it knocked the heart, the real heart, oot of the village. The community of it has gone, the nature of it has gone. We opposed Category D from day one, but it took a hell of a long time to beat.

"They needn't have pulled Wooley Terrace down. It could have been repaired. It was built on the same model as Temperance Terrace (in Grahamsley, a bit further down the hill) and that's still fine. Nee one wanted to help Stanley."

He's in good fettle, he says, spends much of his time reading and thinking, remains a compelling talker. "When he has something to say he usually thinks about it first," Doris had once said. "With a lot of people it's the same thing over and over. That's just rhetoric."

His 380-page book, called *The Flying Pickets* and written with four others, was about the 1972 building workers' strike, the use of "lump" labour and the fate of the so-called Shrewsbury 32, finally acquitted in 2020 after many – including Ricky Tomlinson, the actor – had served jail sentences. "It was elation, real elation," says Dave.

What of Boris? "Nee comment, that's what comes of privilege. That's how he got his job. Totally incapable; terrible."

And of the Labour Party, of which he was once a member? "No comment again. I was a member for a good while but Doris and I had to come out. It has to be the party of change, real change, but it hasn't happened. It isn't a reforming party at all."

We sit socially distanced beneath the brolly for nearly two hours. There's no coal fire, no view across to Yorkshire, but Dave professes himself happy. "Mebbe we haven't won them all, but you can't, can you?" With great good wishes, his birthday card's in the post.

10: United front

July 29 2021

To suggest that Stanley United punched above their weight might be akin to supposing that Muhammad Ali was a half-decent scrapper.

Pitched against the populous, prosperous likes of Bishop Auckland and Crook Town, of Spennymoor United and (whisper it) of Shildon, the village side from the hill top won the Northern League in 1945-46, 1961-62 – when they also lifted the Northern League Challenge Cup with a 5-1 thrashing of West Auckland - and again in 1963-64.

In November 1954 they'd reached the first round of the FA Cup, what football calls the competition proper, for the first and only time. Having beaten near neighbours Wolsingham Welfare in the last qualifying round, United hoped for one of the Football League big boys in the next. Instead they were drawn at Crook, less than a couple of miles but 350ft down the hill, losing a thriller 5-3.

Recalling that occasion in its November 2021 issue, the football magazine When Saturday Comes got its Co Durham Stanleys mixed up – by no means the first and almost certainly not the last to do so – prompting several letters and many more memories.

"Stanley United is one of the oldest and coldest clubs in the North-East," said *Northern Goalfields*, the Northern League's centenary history, in 1989. "Even when it was freezing there was a warmth about the place" says Vince Kirkup, for nearly 30 years the club's dynamo, no less succinctly.

"Stanley might not have had razzmatazz," he'd observed on an earlier occasion, "but it had charm."

Vince loved the place. "On a fine day, you could stand in the centre circle and see the cliffs at Saltburn, or the smoke from the cooling towers at ICI Wilton." Even on a fine day, it might myopically be added, some of us would struggle to see the corner flag.

Until 1974 the Northern League was officially and affirmatively amateur. Like almost all the other clubs, Stanley United were not, players limping not from post-match chilblains or some such podiatric pestilence but from the pound notes shoved surreptitiously into their boots.

Old men in those parts still have nightmares about a knock on the door from the Revenue, or from what Durham miners called the Nash – you know, the National Insurance – demanding their cut of the boot money, and probably with compound interest. Shamateurism, they called it.

Tyneside-based centre forward Geoff Strong, who went from Stanley to Arsenal in 1957, once told me that he'd earned £10 a week, plus £1 a goal – it really was in his boot - on the hill top and £12 a week, then the maximum wage, at Highbury. At Arsenal, of course, it was taxed. He got more for kicking about at Stanley and, unsurprisingly, loved it there.

"Mind, it was the cardest place on earth" said Geoff, reprising his native Newcastle accent and incorrigibly recalling the old joke about Geordie asking his mate to name a card game. "Ice hockey" says his pal.

"That's not a card game" says Geordie.

"Aye it is," insists his mate, "it's the cardest game aa knaa, any

Rust to rust, goal posts and scratching shed

road."

Geoff's view that United's exposed ground represented absolute zero is shared by former England amateur international Dave Rutherford, known universally as Jock, a nomadic Northern League player for almost 30 years. Jock recalls a perishing Hill Top afternoon – "it was probably September" – in his days with Whitby Town.

"We had a lad called Billy Theaker, a hard man who came from Staithes so he knew all about storms. He came off at half-time and he was literally purple, couldn't stop shaking. Eventually they had to call an ambulance and take him off to hospital. I don't think he played at Stanley again."

It wasn't the play or the players for which Stanley United was most celebrated, however, but for the Little House on the Prairie, coal fired and cold comforting, in which half-frozen footballers would seek sanctuary as desperately and as gratefully as the poor souls clinging to the Durham Cathedral knocker.

"Of all the dressing rooms in non-league football, perhaps the most distinctive," the *Groundhoppers* website once observed and with little threat of contradiction.

The little house – changing rooms on the ground floor, bright blazing tea hut and refuge up the steep wooden stairs – had been built, if not quite designed, in the early 20th century. Home-from-homely, it was unique in football. Out the back was built a little referee's room – that is to say, a little room for referees – on the side was tacked a urinal from which it was possible still to watch the game, though with the ever-present danger of peeing on your boots while doing so. A glorious photograph of a chap peering over the wall is on the cover of a recently published football book, coffee table-sized, and will with luck be in this one. You can't see his boots, though.

The great days didn't last. The pits closed, the shops closed, the crowds dissolved. The last team to bear the name of Stanley United folded in October 2005 after losing all of their first six games in the Crook and District League. "There's just no interest, no youngsters coming through," said Ian Dolan, the secretary.

Briefly the pulse quickened when the name of Stanley Town

© S&G and Barratts/EMPICS Sport

Filling his boots - Geoff Strong

appeared on the Crook and District League fixture list for 2021-22, but it proved once again to be the "other" Stanley. The Crook and District League has a wide embrace.

Vince Kirkup, like Davey Ayre in the previous chapter, has no doubt where responsibility for the demise chiefly lies. "It was Durham County Council, Category D. It ripped the heart out of the village and out of the community, and it eventually killed Stanley United."

United, says the Northern League history, had been formed in 1890 by the amalgamation of Stanley Albion and Stanley Nops, and held full FA membership – the same as Arsenal or Manchester United – for 115 years. "Albion" was straightforward, "Nops" puzzling. What's a nop? It was also the nickname of Middlesbrough Ironopolis. Northern League champions for three successive seasons in the 1890s, but Stanley was built on coal, not iron.

Ray Ion's redoubtable researches produce an 1894 cutting recording the amalgamation of the residual Stanley Nops football club and Stanley Star cricket club – "to be known as the Stanley United Athletic Club." The members, the report added, meant business – "the united clubs intend doing great things in the future."

Soon, at least, they were assiduously fund raising. Little over a year later, September 1895, it was reported that a "large gathering" had attended United's annual concert in the church hall. Councillor Harvey occupied the chair, many sang, Mr A Taylor "ably accompanied" on the piano and Messrs Pallister and Milburn were, apparently, "hosts unto themselves." In the rendition of their comic songs and ditties, the report added, they "convulsed the house with mirth."

Stanley Albion, independent again, had in turn disported themselves in February of the same year, more than 100 gathering at Billy Row infant school for a supper and social evening featuring "a most excellent repast." The light fantastic, the report added, "was enjoyed until a late hour."

Beneath the catch-all heading "Local and general news", a newspaper in March 1898 carried but three short paragraphs. The first noted that John Hardman had been arrested in Edinburgh for the New Year's Day murder of his "paramour", the second that a large number had attended a concert in the church mission hall for Stanley United club funds and the third, perhaps most surprising, that the average age of male deaths in Newcastle workhouse was getting on 85.

United's annual sports began on the cricket field in 1900, the principal events the pony scamper and the 120 yards flat handicap, the only minor historical mystery being how they found a flat 120 yards in Stanley. William Rawe of Bankfoot won the pony scamper, V Bell of Howden-le-Wear was first among 58 entrants in the foot running. In the evening, it was noted, the Peases West Silver Band played for dancing.

By 1915, war notwithstanding, the annual event had burgeoned to "gala, sports and flag day", again with a large attendance but with half the profits going to the Soldiers and Sailors Fund at Peases West. The flat race was worth £15, several hundred pounds these days, won by R Thomas of Waterhouses at minuscule odds of 1-3. By 1919, the event also included a choral contest and a quoits tournament and in 1967 the football club's "development committee" was hosting a whippet racing event in conjunction with Wallsend Whippet Club.

Around 150 entries were received, half from Wallsend, special buses laid on to bring dogs and owners from North Tyneside. "It promises to be the biggest sporting event for a long time in the hilltop village" the report added, perhaps forgetting that it wasn't two minutes since they'd won the Northern League.

Meaning business, United had been swiftly successful, notwithstanding an accident on the way back from West Auckland in 1899 when the team charabanc overturned, injuring several players. They won the Durham Amateur Cup in 1901 and 1906 before joining the Northern League at the second time of asking in 1910. Two years earlier they'd been outvoted by West Auckland and York City. In 1910-11, however, United were "thrown out" of the FA Amateur Cup for reasons unrecorded.

At the club's passionate peak there were elections for the committee and a waiting list thereafter – "it was regarded as an honour," says Vince. In 1945-46 the ladies' committee alone had 11 members, though it was about that time that club secretary Bill Nicholson – he of the Miners Arms, aka Nicky's – was summoned by Durham FA to explain why the referee had been waylaid by a group of irate females with brollies employed for a different purpose from that for which meteorologically they had been made. The explanation appears to have been accepted.

Les Westgarth, a committee member for 60 years and chairman for 40, once recalled that when he joined in 1931 the village had eight teams, mostly connected to its churches. "It was easier getting to be lodge secretary at the pit" said Les, "than getting on the committee at Stanley United."

Thousands would somehow be accommodated. For an Amateur Cup tie against Bromley they sold 1,754 programmes at twopence apiece. Les hoped that such income might be enough to re-roof what he liked to call the "bit stand". Originally roofed, the bit stand precariously remains.

Doreen Jobson remembered that she and her mother would spend Saturday mornings making teas, Saturday afternoons serving them and Saturday evenings washing the mucky kit. "No washing machines in those days, we had a bar of soap apiece and just had to get stuck in. We didn't finish until late in the evening when the strips were all hung out in front of the coal fire to dry."

Ernest Armstrong liked to recall that even in the immediate post-war glory days most of the players were local – though one, he conceded, was from Oakenshaw. Oakenshaw's getting on two miles away.

It may be among United's lesser known claims to fame that in the 9-2 defeat at Billingham Synthonia, April 1953, one of Synners' goals was scored by a brash young Teesside lad called Brian Clough, the only goal of a brief Northern League career. He went on to greater things.

Vince had first become acquainted with the Little House in 1971, against Ferryhill Athletic, though he'd played on the school field a decade earlier when St Joseph's RC primary school in Ushaw Moor – known thereabouts as the Joes – travelled to play Stanley school, known usually as Mount Pleasant.

"I'd no idea where the hell Stanley was," he recalls, as a Roman Catholic might not. "I was centre half, we won, but I don't remember it being cold. It must have been September." He does remember the Ferryhill match. "I was marked by Paddy Burke, a real tough nut from Sunderland. At the end I was so exhausted, I was physically sick."

For many post-war years the committee was led by a triumvirate of retired miner Les Westgarth, the chairman, club secretary George Midgley – who sold insurance for the Co-op – and Frank Hogan, the treasurer, who with his wife Nancy ran the village post office and general dealer's shop.

Les had joined the committee in 1931 – "I got ticed," he'd say – and after 57 years active involvement, familiar in old mac and well-worn wellies, received pre-match long service awards from FA and County FA. The occasion was intended to be a surprise, though he'd been pretextually advised to dress up a bit. "I think there were a few tears," says Vince.

Afterwards there was a bit of a do in Billy Row club, though Les had first gone home to get changed. "You can't take the nets down in your best suit," he said.

Vince and I meet today for a three-hour chat at his house in Crook, followed by a pint and a bite to eat – goodness knows he's earned it – at the local kindergarten, more formally known as Wetherspoons. These days he's a greatly energetic chairman of Crook Town FC, for whom Stanley had been voted out of the Northern League in 1936.

From his desk he produces a couple of photo albums, United dating back to 1907-08 in the Durham Aged Miners Cup, the days when committee men might outnumber players, when smiling was optional but clearly frowned upon, when the trainer might be identified by a once-white towel slung causally over his left shoulder and when the goalie wore a cap the size of one of Grandma Batty's Yorkshire puddings and in the louche manner of the late Bobby Thompson. It's quite possible that, like the Little Waster – or legendary Bishop Auckland goalkeeper Harry Sharratt – the custodian also enjoyed a quick Woodbine when not called into action.

Another photograph shows the 1941-42 side – unlike many clubs, United continued throughout the war – more cups than the Naafi canteen.

There were also huge crowds, excitedly overflowing the place, particularly when Crook Town paid a neighbourly visit. The biggest is said to have been the 4,000 somehow shoehorned in for an FA Amateur Cup quarter-final against Leytonstone. When they again left the Northern League before the start of season 1974-75, having finished bottom the previous season, the last home gate had amounted to £2 37, said to equate to 15 adults and an indeterminate number of kids.

"We charge them a penny or twopence or nowt if they have nowt," George Midgley had said. They re-formed in the Durham and District League, joined the Wearside League in 1992 and – pretty much in the guise of the Gurney Valley Salmon Tin Dribblers for whom Vince had pleaded – abandoned the uphill struggle in the autumn of 2005.

The ground remains abandoned, desolate, almost mournful, the derelict scratching shed and giddy-aunt goalposts a gloomy reminder of happier days. Vince is convinced that, despite a covenant restricting the land to leisure use, it'll soon be a site for more new housing. "We all know that you can overturn covenants. All that history, and it'll become just like anywhere else."

What came to be called shamateurism was nothing new, of course. Back in 1927-28, Durham had suspended more than 350 "amateurs" for receiving what euphemistically was termed "tea money", their eyes having proved substantially bigger than their bellies.

Though resident 12,000 miles away in Australia, Professor Gavin Kitching – born and raised in Fencehouses, Co Durham – published in 2021 an erudite account of the roots of North-East football, called *A Fateful Love*. Fifty of its 250 pages were devoted to what became known as The Crook Town Affair.

It was them who started it as we used (ungrammatically) to say when upbraided for playground skirmishes. Perhaps more to the point, it was Crook who kept on winning things.

Prof Kitching's account includes a number of sworn statements from Northern League players at the time, admitting receipt of illegal payments They included Francis Smith, whose address was given as the Constitutional Club in Crook, who'd played for Stanley United in 1914-15 and received seven shillings a match in addition to his tea allowance and the sixpence he claimed for travel between Crook and Stanley.

A sixpenny bus fare in 1914? Like Billy Row bank, it seems a bit steep.

Mind, Smith later received 12/6d a match when playing for Willington in 1921-22 – including travel expenses from Crook, no further than Stanley and no more greatly on the level – and subsequently boasted of a £2 match fee when playing for Bishop Auckland in a Durham Benevolent Bowl tie against Stockton.

Prof Kitching notes that, at much the same time, a Co Durham miner would earn about £2 4s a week and a shipwright £2 15s 7d. A pint of milk was threepence, a white loaf fourpence ha'penny and, in Crook, an unemployed miner with six kids might receive 36 shillings a week dole money.

A Fateful Love addresses all manner of questions. One of those it doesn't is how on earth the likes of Stanley United found the money.

Though Stanley were never a Colliery Welfare club, Vince reckons that income came mainly from the miners of Wooley and, later, of Stanley Drift – that and the Friday night draw which took place between turns at Billy Row workmen's club.

"At lots of the pits the miners would have twopence taken off their notes for the football team, twopence for the band, twopence for the ambulance brigade or whatever. Frank Hogan would give a really good meat parcel for the draw, though there were maybe a dozen other prizes, and then in those days there were good crowds. There was plenty of money."

Further sponsorship had come during and after World War II from Tommy Horn, who owned the celebrated Laurel Toffee factory in Crook. United had continued to play during the conflict. "Sweet rationing was very severe," it's recalled. "Tommy would come up laden with tins of all sorts. It wasn't hard to get men to play for Stanley, especially those with kids."

In 1971, Vince had earned £2 a game – still in an "amateur" league. "It wasn't bad in those days, about £30 in today's money, I only got £2 19s 11d when I started work as an apprentice." Though the toffee ration, what might be supposed a sweetener, was no more, those who'd played well would be offered extra pie and peas in the Little House.

"I'd give £1 to my mam which invariably she'd spend on a packet of Capstan or Senior Service," he recalls. When he returned to Stanley as a player in 1975, and after he became team manager in 1977, the crowds and the money were dwindling pretty much proportionately.

At the start of the 1977-78 United had been unable to raise a team – "I wondered why I hadn't heard anything," says Vince – so was surprised one evening to answer a knock on the door at home in Durham to find George Midgley on the step, on his way to a Durham and District League meeting to resign membership and fold the club.

Before ever George reached the meeting, the decision had been reversed and Vince, then just 27, was manager. "I must have had mug written all over my forehead," he supposes. "I pulled 12 players together in two weeks and our first game was at Blackhall. We only lost 3-nowt."

Partly the financial problem was addressed by his own fund raising efforts at the National Coal Board's workshops at Tursdale, near Ferryhill, where he worked. "It helped that I was the union secretary as well," he admits.

Soon – and for many years thereafter - he was club secretary, just the fourth since 1890, treasurer, kit washer and groundsman as well, chiefly because there was no one else. "I never called myself chairman, I don't know why," he muses. "I guess it was because I was only chairing myself."

Vince finally left in 2002. "I'd had several offers to manage other clubs, about six times from Crook Town alone. Finally I gave in; there just seemed to be nothing more I could do."

As with Dr Johnson's famed aphorism that when two Englishmen meet they talk about the weather, so it's impossible to talk for ten minutes about Stanley United without returning to the self-evident observation that it can get a bit parky up there. Vince reckons that the worst month is February, though it was

on January 31 1948 – near enough frozen February, anyway, the occasion earlier acknowledged – that the ill wind proved most malevolent.

United hosted Yorkshire Amateurs, from Leeds, in the FA Amateur Cup, the storm so severe that four players left the field, unable any longer to stand the cold. All were from Stanley. The Amateurs won 4-1, a cold comfort penalty notwithstanding. David Armstrong, featured in an earlier chapter, was an 11-year-old spectator.

"The cold was appalling but there must have been a dispute at half-time between the players and the committee because four just refused to come back out. To this day I can still see Cherry Brown, one of Stanley's supposed hard men, standing in front of the Little House, bawling, pleading and virtually commanding the others to come off. To their credit, they stayed."

Things that afternoon had also been pretty bleak up at East Tanfield, near the bigger but no more clement Stanley, the tie with Moor Green abandoned when two of the home side and six of the visitors prematurely bolted for the dressing room.

History all but repeated itself at Stanley on November 17 1962 when United played Whitby Town, trailing 2-1 in what *Northern Goalfields* called "Arctic conditions" when five players – again all from the home side – left the field. Cold feet? Laws of the game ordain a minimum seven players, however half-perished. The ref abandoned the match with United losing 2-1.

Something similar had happened at Chilton, a few miles east, in 1930. Though their team led 6-0 against Stockton, four Chilton players hurried from the pitch, frozen, after 65 minutes. The score had somehow reached 7-4 when another Chilton player collapsed, literally blue, perhaps purple, with cold. The match was abandoned. It was Easter weekend.

Vince Kirkup reckons that in nearly three decades up there, they never once lost a player for reasons of exposure. Global warming, he supposes. "Once there'd be falls of snow which lasted for three months, now there's much less and it doesn't last three days. Mind, it's still as cold as ever, and as windy. That hasn't changed at all."

The closest they came to wipe-out may have been in a Wearside League game against Wingate. "The pitch runs north-south and in all those years I've only once known the wind blow in any other direction than from the north. You know how bitter the north wind can be.

"This day the gale, the sleet, everything was hurling in our faces from the north. Keith Burn, one of our players, came off at half-time and his lips were literally blue – he couldn't even drink his tea and nor could many of the others because their hands were shaking so much. It was 0-0, the ref abandoned it and I was a bit upset because we'd have had everything at our backs in the second half. Keith Burn was grateful, though – and I still had to take his boots off for him."

Noteworthy - ground hoppers at Stanley United. Photo from Life's A Ball 90s by Zak Waters and Ivor Baddiel (Fistful of Books)

If it wasn't freezing, blowing a blizzard or essaying a passable impression of Hurricane Charley, the problem with Stanley was the fog. John Morton, 50 years in refereeing, recalls a match on the hill top – "September, mind" – at which George Midgley had offered the warm welcome, figuratively or otherwise.

"He told me they'd sorted out the bath in the ref's room specially for me. I looked at it and there was a 6-inch slug. George picked it up, threw it out and pointed at the corner. They had a new bar of Palmolive."

He also recalls that Stanley Derby Rangers, a local league side based at the Earl Derby pub, played in an all-black strip. "Lovely kit," says John, "but I don't know how they got away with it. The referee had to wear a different coloured top."

Anyway, back to a sunny September afternoon at Stanley United. "George had chucked the slug out and I was getting changed when there was a knock on the door and a chap saying I'd better come and have a look outside. I went out and a lovely day had changed just like that. You literally couldn't see a hand in front of you because of the fog.

"I called the match off and half an hour later there was bright sunshine. That's Stanley for you – and the only consolation is that Tow Law's exactly the same."

One more story – Stanley United v Dunston Federation Brewery, Durham Challenge Cup in the year 2000. United, again struggling for a team, have recruited the diminutive former miner Alan Shoulder, 47, affectionately remembered at Newcastle United and for helping Northern League side Blyth Spartans reach the FA Cup fifth round in 1979.

"The fog and rain were horrible, the worst I've seen even at Stanley United," says Vince.

Shoulder, hard as a three-foot seam but a generally gentle chap, is marked by Paul Brown – known as Porky – one of the Northern League's more combative characters. Towards half-time it all kicks off. Brown is said to have threatened Shoulder with what Her Majesty's courts call grievous bodily harm; Shoulder responds with two quick blows to the chin – what Stanley lads term getting in the first bat and nothing to do with cricket. Both are sent off.

"You're 47, you're too old to be fighting," says Chris Murphy, the referee.

"Aye, and I'm too old to getting a bloody good hiding, an' all," says Alan.

The altercation continues in the Little House and overflows into the car park. "I don't go around looking for trouble but if trouble comes looking, I won't run away," adds Alan, afterwards.

Vince Kirkup has witnessed it all. "In pitman's terms," he says, "Porky Brown got his bait put up."

The little photograph albums are rich with well-remembered names and half-forgotten faces. None stirs fonder memories than the late Geoff Strong. There are men like Jack Howarth, who went on to play more than 400 games for Aldershot, like Billy Bell – to become one of the most successful managers in Northern League history – and Billy Blenkiron, a centre half who had a long first class cricket career with Warwickshire.

There are Dickie and Norman Smart, whose goals helped win the league championship in 1946, Bob Thursby who became an FA Amateur Cup winner with Bishop Auckland while still

View from the Loo. Photo from Life's a Ball 90s by Zak Waters and Ivor Baddiel (Fistful of Books)

in his teens and Tommy Cummings who, after a season with Stanley in the late 1950s became a legendary figure at Burnley, making almost 500 appearances, winning three England B caps and, so much a Lancashire lad by that time that he ran several pubs in the area.

Tommy, as an earlier chapter noted, was to be star attraction when Stanley held a reunion, at Billy Row Club, in 1992. That it was turned nine o'clock before he turned up caused some consternation. Like many more before and since, he'd gone to the wrong Stanley.

On Tommy's recommendation, he was replaced at the heart of defence by Ronnie Tunstall who came from Sunderland, became club captain and married Jean Armstrong, one of that great Stanley dynasty. Jean, sadly, died in July 2021 as this book was being written.

Allan Ball, a United goalkeeper in the 1960s, was a South Hetton miner signed by the Scottish League side Queen of the South in the pit canteen at 2am, first of a succession of North-East players who crossed the border to join the Dumfries club. "If we'd wanted a team of Geordies," someone wrote to the local paper, "we could have got Jayne Middlemiss."

Allan made a record 819 appearances for Queen of the South, 507 of them consecutively, became one of only two Englishmen (and the only former Stanley United player) ever to represent the Scottish League and in his long career was booked just once, by legendary referee Tom "Tiny" Wharton in a match on December 25. The goalie, it's said, had taken profane exception to one of Wharton's decisions – booked for blasphemy on Christmas Day. He ran a garage business in Dumfries and died there, aged 75, in 2018.

Doug Raine, who captained the successful 60s' side, was a council binman, reckoned the hardest bloke in the Northern League – a competition not known for its softies – but a perfectly pleasant chap once the final whistle blew. He was also reputed twice to have been banned *sine die*, a conundrum for the classicists. The only opponent ever to scare the life out of him, it's reckoned, was "Big" Billy Wright, Whitley Bay's seismic centre forward. Suffice that, after one occasion when irresistible force had met immoveable object, Doug was said to have locked himself in the dressing room, the Big Bad Wolf hammering on the door and threatening to blow the house down.

Geoff Strong was before Vince's time, though the stories have been passed down. "Apparently he came as a full back, played one game and was useless. The next match they only had 11 men and no centre forward so they put him up front because he couldn't do any worse. The rest is history."

Arsenal paid £100 – in two measly instalments – plus a set of white shirts. The new man scored on his Gunners debut, a 5-1 win against Newcastle United – his home town club – having replaced the famously acerbic Tommy Docherty. "I can still hear Tommy's language," he said. After the match he was embraced by Jimmy Scoular, the Magpies' granite skipper. "You're going to be a good player, son" said Scoular and may never have spoken a truer word.

For a wonderfully successful Liverpool side he played in every outfield position – "a serial chameleon," said one of the obituaries, and a lovely feller, too.

Among all of them, however, my favourite may have been Harry Clarke (1921-2015) who not only played both football and cricket for Durham County but was credited – like many more,

Flag day....

it should be said – with being father of the phrase about its being black over Bill's mother's. Harry denied paternity, claimed that it was someone from Shildon, reckoned – scandalously – that they did some weird and wonderful things in Shildon.

He had three spells with Darlington, transferred between the first and second of them to Leeds United for what back then was termed a consideration but was reckoned £6,000. "I think Leeds thought I'd improve," he said. "I didn't."

In his first Darlington spell he also claimed to have scored five, all headers, in a wartime game. Records, however, suggest that two of them were penalties, adding hitherto unimagined artifice to the spot kicker's craft. He lived in Darlington, bore in later years a passing resemblance to Private Godfrey from *Dad's Army*, had framed on the wall a poem written in honour of his third coming to Feethams:

This is the tale of the man who came back

When everyone said he was finished,

He was getting too old and getting too fat

And the force of his football diminished....

It may also have been the only poem in history to find a rhyme for opportunist – cartoonist. Darlington paid him £5 a week, Leeds £8. On Stanley Hill Top his riches may have been unimagined but were also unrecorded. Just one thing's certain: if he'd played today, Harry Clarke would have been worth a fortune.

Bob Thursby was just 18, in his first year at dental school in Newcastle and already an England youth international when persuaded to sign for Stanley. A year later he joined Bishop Auckland, with whom he won England amateur honours and an FA Amateur Cup winner's medal.

"No offence to the Bishops," he says, "but that year at Stanley was probably the happiest of my football life. Fabulous people, the salt of the earth."

He lived in Chester-le-Street, picked up on match days by a taxi paid for by the club. "I'd often be there first, sitting huddled over the fire with my duffel coat still on and the hood up. One of the committee would come in and say what a nice day it was."

He'd once been down the pit with a youth club party. "I saw for myself how tough and horrible the working conditions were. Most of the Stanley committee were miners and I think part of the reason they were involved was for the fresh air.

"The facilities were pretty basic, the communal bath like a horse trough, but the women's committee were wonderful and the food the best in the Northern League. I used to get seconds, probably because I was the youngest. I'd have gone there just for the teas."

He also remembers the treasurer, though not his name. "He had wash leather trouser pockets, carried every penny they had around with him. I'd be paid a few bob, I was just a poor student, but I don't think it was a fortune."

The club were also full members of the Football Association, allowed a small annual allocation of FA Cup final tickets – usually the more expensive sort. "Someone arranged to swap them for a load of 3/6d tickets and the club took all the players down to the final. Birmingham v Manchester City, on the bus.

"They put us up in digs owned by the National Union of Mineworkers near Kings Cross, took us out for meals, the lot. We had a great weekend at the Cup final and it didn't cost me a penny. That's what's called looking after your players."

Bob also recalls Stanley team mate Gordon Bradley, Sunderland lad and Easington collier, who after time in the Football League became player and then manager of New York Cosmos, signed the likes of Pele, Cruyff and Carlos Alberto, picked himself for the USA when appointed national team manager, became a well-known television commentator and was instituted into the US Soccer Hall of Fame.

Gordon died in 2008, aged 74. How much of his success was

Framed- the team circa 1980; Vince Kirkup bottom left

STANLEY UNITED F.C. SPORTS.

The first annual gala and sports in connection with the Stanley United Football Club took place on the Cricket Field, Stanley, Crook, on Saturday. There was a capital attendance. The principal events of the afternoon were the pony scamper and the flat handicap. The results were as follows:—Pony scamper: 1, Wm Rawe, Bankfoot, Crook; 2. Wm Snowdon, Billy Row. Flat handicap: There were about 58 entries. The handicapper was Mr R Stoker; pistol firer, Mr C Jones; judge, Mr R Smith. Final: 1. V Bell, Howden (12½yds); 2, J Winter, Crook (13½); 3, W Hall, Waterhouses. Other sports took place, and in the evening the Pease West Silver Band played for dancing.

THE STANLEY ALBION FOOTBALL CLUB.

On Friday evening, under the auspices of the Stanley Albion Football Club, a most successful supper and social gathering was held in the Infant School, Billy Row, when over 100 assembled, and partook of an excellent repast. The following ladies presided at the tables: Mesdames W. Greggor, W. Neil, P. Garr, and Misses Reid, Dunn, and Greggor. To the music of Mr T. Robinson and W. Moyser, the light fantastic toe was enjoyed until a late hour. Among those present were noticed Mr and Mrs T. Robinson, Mr and Mrs Kidd, Mr and Mrs W. Westgarth, Mr and Mrs G. Westgarth, Mr and Mrs W. Pinkney, Miss M. Cragg, Miss Watson (Sunniside), Miss Dale and Miss Claxon, Messrs W. Betton, R. Peacock, J. Coates, T. Cragg, W. Cragg, C. Pearson, J. Scales, and others.

FOOTBALL CONCERT AT CROOK.

On Monday there was a large assembly in the Church Hall, Stanley, where the Stanley United Football Club were holding their annual concert. Councillor Harvey occupied the chair, and the following vocalists sustained a conspicuous part in the programme:—Miss Richards, Miss Rowland, Messrs Ed. Milburn, Wm Pallister, J. Richards, J. Williams, R. Young, Robinson and W. Mawson. Mr A. Taylor, of Crook, ably accompanied on the piano. Messrs Pallister and Milburn were a host in themselves. In the rendition of their comic songs and ditties they convulsed the house with mirth. The vocalists throughout were well received and were rewarded by loud applause and frequent recalls.

STANLEY UNITED.

Largely influenced by acute industrial conditions, Stanley United Football Club showed a loss on the past season of £11 2s. 10½d. The income amounted to £223 11s. 1½d., and the expenditure £234 14s. At the annual meeting it was reported that before the season started the adverse balance would in all probability have been wiped out.

Cutting remarks....

down to that formative time on the Hill Top was, sadly, never recorded.

Billy Roughley, himself an England amateur international, played for Bishop Auckland and won an Amateur Cup winner's medal with Crook Town – to whom Stanley were always the old enemy. Affectionately, he also remembers the post-match food at the Little House on the Prairie. "When I went with Bishop Auckland we'd get a tremendous spread. When I went with Crook we were lucky to get a sandwich."

Vince Kirkup had just returned from holiday, late one night in 2007, when a telephone call informed him of a big fire at the Little House. "I thought I'd seen a glow in the sky," he recalls. "It went up like an oil well. The walls were just tongue and groove wood, if a bit fell off it turned to dust. The floors were wooden, too, no wonder it burned. It was absolutely soul destroying."

The arsonists had got in through the ref's room. Though several callers offered names and addresses of the supposed culprits, no arrests were made.

Marking its centenary, the football club had bought the ground from the Coal Industry Social Welfare Organisation in 1990, a deal which took Vince two years to negotiate. "They valued it at £30,000, just for the grazing rights," he says. "I showed them the books, we had £245. We could never have found the money."

Instead the Coal Board offered to sponsor United for £29,999, the remaining £1 handed over in a centre circle ceremony which got in the *Daily Express* on the Monday morning. Conditions included not just the stipulation that the ground continue to be used for sport but that any football team be called Stanley United.

In 1984 the club had re-joined the Wearside League. In 1996 – a nod to the past, High Road again wick with folk – they hosted a match against South Bank in the Northern League's final ground hoppers weekend, a five-year exercise embracing 43 clubs, all but one in the Northern League itself. At the end of it all, the travellers were invited to vote for their favourite venue. Stanley won by the length of Windy Ridge.

In May 2003, club and clubman departed, Crook Wanderers ventured up the hill to take over ground and name and to assume the salmon tin dribblers role. It didn't last: only horses, perhaps the odd goat, are up there now. Vince, the ground's sole trustee, had sold it back to the coal industry's social welfare arm and got the asking price, his pound back. "I certainly didn't want to make a profit," he says. "I love it at Crook Town, I'll do anything for them, but I still miss Stanley United.

"There was a camaraderie about it, we had nowt but I enjoyed it. Mind, if I'd stopped there much longer, I think it would have killed me."

11: doubting St Thomas

August 5 2021

First the good news: a statement today advises that after nearly18 months of Covid-conditioned closure. St Thomas's church will resume regular Sunday services on August 15, once a month at 10am. The bad news – "bitter-sweet", the statement concedes – is that it's likely to close permanently after Christmas.

Jonathan Kindleysides, the church council secretary, points out that once there were eight churches and chapels in the barely-divisible little villages between Crook and Tow Law. If St Thomas's closes there'll be none, the rumour of God ever more muted.

It's not unexpected. Back in 1979, the *Evening Despatch* reported that St Thomas's faced bills of several thousand pounds to repair damage caused by "severe winter weather". Three years later, *The Northern Echo* claimed that "the cathedral on the hill" faced closure as congregations ever-dwindled. Numbers on the electoral roll had fallen to seventy – seventy! – while there were no more than twenty (twenty!) Sunday regulars.

An 1898 report, thanks again to Ray Ion, recorded the election of two churchwardens and no fewer than 17 sidesmen, adding that the previous year's income amounted to £89 14s. Over 70 members had also had "a jolly time" at the Church Institute Industrial Improvement Society, another "excellent repast" and a lecture on phrenology, which among so abstemious a number is unlikely to have gone to the head. Waiters and waitresses were named, Mr John Stoker undertook "onerous duties" and "games were freely indulged in until a very late hour."

At the Primitive Methodists, meanwhile, the Band of Hope members had been entertained to tea. Anniversary events continued with "very well attended" services and a Monday evening concert. "Great praise was bestowed on little Miss Hodgson who contributed largely to the harmony of the evening and sang 'My darling doll'."

Clearly it was all happening on the Hill Top.

The cover of a 1923 parish magazine, posted on the "*If you lived in Stanley….*" Facebook page listed St Thomas's Sunday services at 10 30am and 6pm, young men's Bible class at 1 45pm, Sunday School 2 30pm, baptisms on Sundays at 3 30pm and Wednesdays at 6 30pm and a seven o'clock prayer meeting on Wednesdays.

Four "parochial readers" – unpaid lay ministers – included Tommy Horn, the Laurel Toffee maker who'd also befriended Stanley United – with enough sidesmen to turn out two football teams. Sunday services also included a 6pm "mission church" at Sunniside, part of the Stanley parish but a mile westwards. The mission church, says Jonathan, was looked after by the curate, who lived in Sunniside. The church building survives, but is now Waggott's garage.

Back in 2001, I'd attended the closing service at Billy Row Methodist church which in the mid-19th century had held services in both English and Welsh, in order to accommodate the burgeoning immigrant workforce. Someone produced a Crook Methodist Circuit "plan" from 50 years earlier, when the circuit had three ministers and 17 churches – two in Tow Law, two in Stanley, two in Billy Row and others in places like Roddymoor and Sunniside. Now there isn't even a Crook circuit.

Ernest Armstrong had preached at the final service at Mount

Pleasant Methodist church – originally Primitive Methodist – in Stanley in June 1966. Closure was blamed on "a combination of circumstances", perhaps one of them that Wooley Terrace chapel, built for £600 after two years fund raising, was barely a quarter of a mile away. Though Methodism's two wings has formally united in 1932, Wooley Terrace was still regarded as

Gutted – the burned out St Thomas's

Wesley Methodist. Mount Pleasant members were simply told that they could attend Wooley if they wished.

In a sense that sad Sunday in Billy Row was like attending the funeral of an old miner whose workmates had long predeceased him, a brave and upbeat occasion though moist eyes could not entirely be blamed upon the menthol and eucalyptus sweets, surreptitiously rustled around and overpowering from three pews back.

David Armstrong prayed that witness in "God's own country" might continue up the bank at Wooley Terrace, where Doreen Ainsley had pretty much quoted Matthew: 9 about the harvest being plenteous but the workers having downed tools. Readers know already what happened at Wooley Terrace.

St Thomas's, now a Grade II listed building, cost £3,162 when opened in February 1877. Slightly out of Stanley, on the road to Sunniside, it could seat 500 and hoped to attract worshippers from both villages. Known originally as Mount Pleasant church, part of Brancepeth parish, it was renamed Stanley Crook by the Diocese of Durham – so they're to blame – once again in a futile attempt to avoid confusion.

In November 1893, however, the church was severely damaged by fire during a storm so severe that the heating system exploded. It was reopened a year later – at much the same time that the church hall burned down. "The church has not had a quiet history, in fact rather a turbulent one," says its website, and rarely more turbulent than when Dr David Jenkins, the former Bishop of Durham, preached at an International Workers' Memorial Day service in 2005.

The annual service was promoted by Dave Ayre, marked

globally but rarely with more passion than on the hill top. "Mourn the dead, fight for the living," ordained the watchword, engraved also on a Workers' Memorial window dedicated at the church in 2002 after the original window had been blown in by a 90mph gale. A banner carried into church promoted "Socialism" and "revolution"; inevitably, perhaps, we sang about fighting the good fight.

Though long a member of the House of Lords, Dr Jenkins was very much one of the workers, as miners striking in 1983 could with almost religious fervour attest. "Today," he told his Stanley congregation, "the most obvious and chief reason for not believing in God is the words and actions of those who say that they do."

The sermon deserved a larger audience than those gathered in St Thomas's on a characteristically chilly evening, the bishop anxious to warm them. "Though in my 81st year and fed up with religious and religion," he said, "I can't for the life of my stop believing in God."

The fire still burned in Dave Ayre, too.

A couple of years earlier, Bishop Gary Weatherill had flown 12,000 miles from Queensland to Co Durham for Fr Peter Davis's first profession to monastic orders. When the bishop had left Queensland it had been 105 degrees Fahrenheit; in Stanley it was 38 degrees and falling fecklessly. We'd mentioned Fr Peter in the opening chapter, blown into the parishes around Tow Law, Stanley and Satley like the blizzard of Oz, though there'd still be folk up there who supposed the outback to be the netty.

It was Martin Luther King Day. If the young Peter Davis had had a dream all those years ago back in Australia, it probably wasn't that he'd find himself prostrate on Windy Ridge, taking monastic vows.

A member of the Society of the Sacred Mission, he not only had a voracious appetite but was known even to stand his round in the pub – an act believed by some Church of England clergy to be a breach of at least five of the 39 Articles of Religion. Sadly he left two years later, citing ill health.

On another occasion, in 2015, I'd been at St Thomas's for a performance of *Messiah* – one of Christendom's great musical works in one of its great little churches – by the Crook and Weardale Choral Society, black-tied and formal and considerably outnumbering the audience. Altogether less formal, the audience remained top coated. It was only May, after all.

The statement on St Thomas's future is blunt. During 2020, when the church effectively closed for nine months, it still cost £4,962 to run. Income from occasional services – like funerals – and from donations totalled just £2,266. "Clearly this is an unsustainable situation," the statement adds. "The pandemic has been the last straw."

Over 20 years, it supposes, a regular congregation of about eight people has kept the church "plodding along." Just eight? There's a photograph on the internet somewhere of St Thomas's choir, probably between the wars, with more than 20 robed boy choristers alone (and the vicar looking suitably miserable). "Oh aye," says Dave Ayre, "singing in that choir was regarded as an honour."

Now some, like Dave and Doris Ayre, are no longer regularly able to attend because of health issues. The website quotes the final lines of John Betjeman's poem Verses Turned, on the decline of the Church of England:

And must that plaintive bell in vain

Peal loud along the dripping lane?

And must the building fall?

Not when we love the church and live

And of our charity will give

Our much, our more, our all.

"St Thomas's has never been a wealthy parish," the statement adds, "always having a hand to mouth existence. With a congregation of no more than nine, on a good day, having a huge building like this can no longer be justified. Unfortunately the state and size of the building does not readily lend itself to other community uses.

"It will break the hearts of the congregation to close the doors for the last time but a small congregation can no longer bear the burden of funding and maintaining a building that so few want to use."

Though a final decision hasn't yet been taken, it's expected that the church will close in January. Before that a "huge" Christmas service is planned. Even before that, I'll be heading back to the hill top on Sunday August 15.

12: Sunday best

August 15 2021

There's a very early (and not very artful) Simon and Garfunkel track, circa 1965, on which the long-discordant duo sing *Silent Night* against the doleful background of the Six O'clock News. Vietnam and all that, probably. Today's a bit like that.

The 9am news is on the car radio as we head up the A68 towards Stanley: Taliban terrorising Afghanistan, gun massacre in Plymouth, earthquake disaster in Haiti. On top of that it's mizzling, drizzling and worsening by the mile the closer we get to St Thomas's.

Doubting Thomas? How could he?

We're on the Hill Top by 9 35am, preceded only by the Rev Geoff Lawes, outside in the porch and ministering to a tortoiseshell butterfly which seems similarly to be suffering life expectancy issues. "She looks a bit exhausted," he says.

Mr Lawes is 84, had been both a priest and teacher on South Tyneside before becoming Vicar of Annfield Plain and Annfield Colliery in north-west Durham. "The colliery end of the parish hardly exists," he says. He and his wife moved to Crook, he assuming an honorary role across the five churches of the extended Wolsingham parish. His wife's what they call a reader, an unpaid lay minister.

He talks about how he particularly loves St Thomas's, says he wants his funeral to be held there, acknowledges what might be termed a potential conflict of interest. Which of them will go first, he or the beloved church?

Though it's said that folk can see for many a mile from the church gate, today you can hardly make out the sheep, safely grazing in the field across the road. The bus timetable on the post outside reveals that, like St Thomas's for the previous 17 months, there are no Sunday services. Ecclesiastically, at any rate, it's about to change.

Though clearly in need of more TLC than in recent times has been possible, it's a lovely church full of character (if no longer full of characters.) Kitchen and toilets are relatively new, attributed to Dave Ayre's tireless fund raising to mark the Millennium.

The Wooley Colliery lodge banner stands squarely behind the altar cross – in what other church might that happen? – while the banner of the Crook branch of the Union of Construction and Technical Trades, the one that proclaims Socialism and revolution, leans on the south wall close to the International Workers' Memorial window.

The opening line of an Easter hymn springs to mind: the strife is o'er, the battle won. Not just yet, maybe.

On the walls elsewhere are photographic collages of Stanley's past, sometimes up to the oxters in snow and often featuring the miners, coal-scarred and cloth capped. Alongside the pews, large numbers of piled chairs speak of the triumph of optimism over realism but when folk claim, as still they do, that the Church of England is the Conservative Party at prayer, they really should get themselves to St Thomas's.

It's a community church, a people's church, the wretched thing that so few people now appear called to it. Still a band of hope? "I don't think we'll ever again have a time when many come regularly," concedes Jonathan Kindleysides. "Most people still want it to be here for their own purposes, weddings and funerals, but they're not prepared to help financially or sometimes to turn up on Sundays. Unless a millionaire comes along, I don't think we'll be opening after Christmas."

Another problem, Jonathan concedes, is that in winter it can get awfully cold in there. Truth to tell, it's by no means shirtsleeve weather, even in mid-August. There's a limit to what can be achieved, especially on the Hill Top, with a three-bar electric fire, a bit of good faith and a ganzey.

"It's not really suitable for community use, particularly in winter," says Jonathan. "Stanley has a very good village hall and we don't want to muscle in on that, especially when it's cold."

Since news of the likely closure appeared on social media ten days previously, he's had £500 in donations – "most of it from people I'd never heard of" – while Geoff Lawes took a call from a former Crook resident now in the Czech Republic offering a regular donation for as long as the church remained open.

"It was greatly kind," says Mr Lawes. "I just don't know for how long he'll have to keep on giving."

It's the Feast of the Blessed Virgin Mary. The 15 or so folk scattered around the church include us two and four or five children with their parents – "twice as many here as usual, that's good" says Mr Lawes. Probably because of Covid concerns, Dave and Doris Ayre can't make it. Singing's accompanied not by the organ but by a music machine, somewhere at the back, with little regard for harmony – or, at least, not the same harmony as the rest of us.

The first hymn's *Morning has broken*. "Mine is the sunlight, mine is the morning; Born of the one light, Eden saw play."

However more meteorologically appropriate, they could hardly start with "All is safely gathered in (ere the winter storms begin)."

Mr Lawes reports that he has had a "warming" letter from the archdeacon and a "down to earth" discussion about the church's future. Among the problems, he says, is an annual insurance bill exceeding £2,000 and due – "of all days" – on December 25. The church fabric isn't good either, he adds.

It's without intended offence to the sermon, on the Blessed Virgin, that half way through I find myself pondering what might be the single word which most appropriately would describe the preacher. Perhaps for the first time ever, I come up with mannerly. Certainly he is gentlemanly, scholarly and clearly

Rooms with a view – the Foresters

much respected.

He notes also that it's National Relaxation Day, a snippet which it's to be hoped he gleaned while enjoying a glass of something fortifying in his armchair.

Vera Ryder, 78, was baptised, confirmed and married at St Thomas's, though her family moved down to Billy Row when she was five. As with Geoff Lawes, she hopes that her funeral may also be there but concedes that such circumstances may be beyond her control.

Over coffee after the service she recalls when the Sunday School would have two or three well-attended classes, when the vicar's wife held an embroidery group, when the choir had a waiting list and when even that 500-seat church was "quite full" every Sabbath.

"I'm very sorry about what's happening, but it's the way things are going isn't it? People just won't go to church. I don't think that these days they're so friendly, either. There's not the same neighbourliness; people don't ask how you're getting on any longer."

Someone else points out that three other village churches in the Crook deanery alone – Frosterley, Rookhope and Howden-le-Wear – have closed in recent times. Jonathan Kindleysides wonders if Tow Law might follow them. "They're a bit healthier than we are but not far behind."

Geoff Lawes recalls that when he studied theology at Durham, college contemporaries would be sent to cover services at St George's in Peases West. "When I went to Satley, the prayer book still had 'St George's Peases West' stamped inside."

So what if St Thomas's closes? What if there really are no places of worship between Crook and Tow Law? Can the tide ever be turned, the rumour of God re-amplified? Mr Lawes carefully removes and folds his vestments. "I'm afraid I don't know," he says. The tortoiseshell, the bright elusive butterfly, has flown.

Amens said, coffee quaffed, we head to the other end of the village for Sunday lunch at the Foresters Arms, and are by no means alone. Jim Mulligan, who runs the place with his partner Denise, reckons they'll be serving well over 100 dinners – pork dinners, beef dinners, chicken dinners, gammon dinners – both to eat in and take out. Almost none of his custom is from the village.

"They maybe haven't the money," he muses. "The old houses in Stanley are cheap but the new ones can be very expensive. If you've a big mortgage, there mightn't be a lot left."

As with the panorama from the gate of St Thomas's church, the view would be magnificent if only you could see it. "People talk about the view from the front, but from the side you can see Saltburn cliffs as clear as crystal," says Jim. "They also book the back rooms so they can overlook the garden, The garden's lovely."

These are proper Co Durham Sunday dinners – lunches for those who prefer – the kind of which folk with justification aver that they couldn't make it any cheaper at home. It's also proper Co Durham because there are no starters, because the Yorkshire pudding is served with the meat – no primitive Yorkshire practices here – and because, save for the mushy peas, vegetables are piled together in a separate bowl.

The peas, dense and fragrant and almost bottle green, are piled high in yet another bowl, from which they are extricated with an almost onomatopoeic slurp. As used to be said of Hovis, or some such, it's just as mother used to make.

Options are large or small. Large is £8 50. Real men, or indeed their wives, don't eat small Sunday dinners.

Mostly, however, this is a true Co Dirham occasion because it's top loaded, which is to say that it's chiefly frequented by folk who really do prefer their mid-day meal at noon and then spend

Special guest – Matt Baker

the rest of Sunday afternoon wondering what's for tea.

Sharon – who's Welsh and, well, different – recalls a long-gone Sabbath visit to my folks in Shildon, probably still in our state of unmarried bliss. "They'd not only had their dinner but had done the washing up," she says. It was 11 50am.

It may also be a Co Durham quirk that a chap in the bar asks for a glass of Marlow, as if the wine had come from that well-heeled Berkshire town, while another correctly pronounces Sauvignon blanc but then sups it through a straw.

Over two floors there's just one empty table, and that's the one which holds sundry sanitizers, a reminder that the virus still prowls, like the devil thy adversary, seeking whomsoever it might devour.. Food's served by cheery young ladies, their universally sylph-like frames perhaps encouraged by several flights of stairs, keen to compare GCSE results and to ponder what happens next. Great things, very likely.

With the possible exception of something called Malteser Surprise – a slight surprise is that they still make Maltesers – puddings are traditional, too, and all the more appropriate for that. A replay of *Two Way Family Favourites*, Cliff Michelmore and his missus, would make a nostalgic occasion complete.

Once Stanley had four thirst-slaking pubs – the Heights of Alma, the Earl Derby, open and shut like a wicket gate and thereabouts usually pronounced to rhyme with Furby, the Wooley New Inn (aka the White City) and the Robin Hood, which became the Foresters and is now basically run as a guest house, though with a full licence. Framed on the bar wall, a notice discloses that the former pub sign depicted Robin Hood clad in bright red – the artist may have been colour blind – with

Little John in forest green. Beneath the image were the words:

Gentlemen, my name is good

This is the sign of Robin Hood,

If Robin Hood be not at home

Come and dine with Little John.

The sign was taken down in 1994. Its whereabouts, sadly, are now a mystery.

The New Inn, it's reckoned, was particularly popular in the late evening because, being on the east side of the road up past the school, it was in a different parliamentary and police division and thus – to the considerable frustration of the village bobby – allowed to open half an hour later than those in Stanley itself.

An early 20th century map sent by the incomparable Mr Ion confirms that the road was indeed the boundary of both the parliamentary district and of the union. Whatever the union was, Stanley thirsty miners were keen to be part of it.

Jim Mulligan, now 79, was born up the road in Sunniside, moved around the county – once as far as Bishop Middleham, goodness knows – already ran a nearby skip hire business and garage when the Foresters came on the market in 2009. It had been turned from pub to nursing home.

"Word got around that we were going to turn it into a halfway house for people released from prison," he recalls. "We had to go to all sorts of appeals. There were about 30 objections, led by a polliss who lived a few doors down. A couple of weeks after we got planning permission, he put his house on the market and was off.

"People told us we were crackers, totally crackers, said it would never work. The builders were in seven or eight months, the conversion cost a lot of money, but sometimes you have to be crackers in business, don't you."

He hasn't a mobile phone – "I've had phones ringing in my ears all my life, I don't want any more" – leaves electronic communication to others, fronts the operation with energy and great good grace.

The eight bedroom guest house, he says, was once a staging inn. Photographs of the pub before its transformation show bar, black leaded fireplace – "we kept the frame, couldn't get the black lead off" – and what Co Durham folk used to call the singing end, furnished with a sit-up-and-beg piano. They can still sing if they want, says Jim, but unfortunately they haven't a piano.

Enthusiastically recommended on social media, promoted (not unreasonably) as the gateway to Weardale, it has prospered since lockdown was eased. Regular guests have included BBC *Countryfile* presenter Matt Baker and his family, periodically joined by production team members. Another chap, hospital anaesthetist, stayed for two months and every Saturday walked along the Deerness Valley Way, the old railway lines into Durham. "He couldn't believe how lovely it all was," says Jim.

Other regulars include a couple from Munich and another from the south coast of England who spent two years in France, sought a return to Blighty and could find nowhere on earth that they'd rather be than Stanley Hill Top; Further note to self: try to track down the French connection.

Bookings remain greatly healthy. "It's been brilliant," says Jim. "Why would all those people keep coming back to Stanley? It's simply because they love it."

Local Derby: one of the vanished pubs

13: radio times

August 19 2021

Before the next chapter officially opens, a return to the village hall but on a very different wavelength from the lucky-for-some bingo, there's chance of a teatime dander around the dear village. Though it's still mizzling, the verges are verdant and the wind turbines tranquilised.

Returning commuters have replaced colliery hooters, Sainsbury's van replaced the store horse. One or two of Stanley's long-terraced houses even have conservatories and – if that May-time straw poll in Billy Row Club is to be credited – quite likely Conservatives as well.

The thought again occurs that the village has no notices, save for a couple of hand-written jobs on Mount Pleasant asking that deliveries be taken round the back – two houses have pre-empted the request by bricking up the front door – and the usual stuff from BT, advising in suitable terms where their telegraph poles might be put.

Nothing else; no forthcoming events, not even a missing moggy. It suggests either that this is a place where there's nothing much going on or, if there is, that its light is hidden biblically beneath a bushel.

A sign in the village hall foyer advises that the building's maximum capacity is 175 people, though neither shape nor size is specified. About a tenth of that number are gathered for the weekly Thursday evening meeting of what officially is the Bishop Auckland Radio Amateurs Club but which may more familiarly be known as the hams.

The 1950s comedian Tony Hancock once devoted a Half Hour

to being a radio ham and, very likely, was off-message. I resolve before arrival not to mention *Hancock's Half Hour*. As for *Can You Hear Me Mother....*

The ham stock etymology's interesting, for all that. The most popular theory appears to be that the original "hams", around the turn of the 19th century, were ham-fisted US wireless telegraphists blamed for what the Americans would call several train wrecks. Another claimed explanation is that HAM was simply the call sign of the amateur radio club in Harvard.

Ian Bowman, the Bishop Auckland club chairman, an industrial chemist not an etymologist, proposes something much simpler. "I think it's just the same as amateur dramatics," he says. The term is no longer thought pejorative; it wasn't always the case.

The hobby, self-evidently global, is said to have two million participants. Enthusiasts have ranged from Dr Alex Comfort, who wrote *The Joy of Sex* to Marlon Brando, who probably knew something about such things, too. Others have ranged from Yuri Gagarin to Brian Rix and from King Juan Carlos of Spain to King Hussein (and Queen Noor) of Jordan.

Many on-line accounts talk up Falkland-based amateur operators' role in the 1981 conflict, from relaying bits of useful information back to the UK to practically wiping out the Argentinians single-handedly (a claim about which the late Lady Thatcher may have had something to say.)

Several Bishop Auckland members have hooked up with crew on the International Space Station, one or two found themselves passing the time of day with King Hussein. Joyfully or otherwise, none admits to comparing notes with Dr Comfort.

The club was formed in the 1980s at the Travellers Rest in

Evenwood, a few miles west of Bishop Auckland. When the pub's future was in doubt, a member who'd helped convert the Green Hut at Stanley into the current village hall suggested that it might make a good base. So it has proved, the antenna out the back capable of being extended to 90ft.

The mast was there before most of the surrounding new housing, though – as might be supposed of a radio club – it did attract a slightly mixed reception. "I don't think some of them even noticed it at first and when they did they were quick to ask if we had planning permission," says Ian. "Of course we had."

Does it help having a very high frequency, as might be supposed of a weekly radio club on the hill top? "It certainly makes a difference, We have a lot of short wave bands which are bouncing stuff all around the ionosphere. On top of a hill is a very good place to be."

This evening's very much a social gathering – "putting the world to rights" says the chairman. "Serious" meetings are held monthly. In one corner, it's a social gathering with cakes. "A great big box of cream cakes used to arrive, but I think a few of them had to go on a diet" adds Ian.

At once he also calls up a Facebook page, posted by Karl Utley, promising details of gruesome historical events in the Stanley and Billy Row areas – yet further note to self, try to find Karl Utley – and hands over a couple of back copies of *Radcom*, the magazine of the Radio Society of Great Britain ("advancing amateur radio since 1913"). They could hardly call it *Radio Times*, someone thought of it first.

The mags overflow with ads for all manner of technical gear – t-shirts, too, "May the Morse be with you" – and with features

with headers like "Raspberry Pi explained." Not to me it's not; I haven't even learned, can't begin to imagine, how to write "ionosphere" in shorthand.

Membership's about 40, spread across Co Durham. None is from Stanley. The club offers training at three different levels, from the foundation course – about eight to 15 weeks, a reception class, as it were – to an advanced qualification which allows use of an exclusive call sign. "After that," says Ian, "the world's your oyster."

Members have been as young as eight, one youngster a girl with learning difficulties. "We just took it at her own speed, when she passed she was ecstatic, her parents couldn't get her out of the place."

Tonight the only female member is Kathleen Woodhams from Newton Aycliffe, there with Dudley, her husband. Her father

Aerial view – village hall and radio mast

had been a telegraphist in World War II. "He kept trying to teach me the Morse code," she recalls. "At the age of 18 I said I'd like to get a licence but my mother said there wasn't a cat in hell's chance, She didn't want me up in the attic all hours, like my dad had been."

She and Dudley again switched on to amateur radio in 2013, after becoming interested during a camping trip. Why so few women? "I think it's the technological side," says Kathleen. "Some of it goes over my head a bit, but it's a fascinating hobby and you get to speak to people from all over the world; you never know who's going to pop up – I once found myself talking to someone from Puerto Rico and I didn't even know where Puerto Rico was. It's also a very friendly club."

Kit can cost anything from £50 to five figures. Few this evening have anything in front of them but will have equipment, it's reckoned, in the cars outside. "Tonight they can do pretty much anything they want," says the chairman, though they'd probably draw the line at bingo.

How hard is it to master? "Watch Tony Hancock and you'll find out," says Kathleen, unprompted, and already I've learned enough to guess that she's probably being sarcastic.

As in aviation, English is the international language. That apart, an attempted explanation would be akin to summarising the theory of relatively on the back of a postage stamp. Protocols insist that they don't talk politics, religion or football – some of us would have nowt left to talk about, anyway – and that offensive language is frowned upon. Not like football, then.

Amateur radio enthusiasts are also much involved in the community. In September they'll be helping marshal the Great North Bike Ride from Seahouses to Tynemouth; on the Eden Valley Railway in Cumbria the Bishop Auckland club is so much part of the operation that they have a permanent shack – a radio station – at the terminus at Warcop.

"It can become very addictive but in a positive way," says Brian Phillipson, a radio enthusiast since CB days in the 1970s – "when it was totally illegal," he concedes. Sometimes he might be on the radio three or four hours a day during the week, maybe eight or ten at weekends. It's both learning and enjoyment, he says.

I sign off about 9 15pm, heading down to Crook for the dutiful No 1. Outside it's finally stopped raining – the evening fragrant, the village tranquil, the views of street lights many a mile to the south. The rest is radio silence.

14: naming rights

August 25 2021

Until summarily and wholly unexpectedly defenestrated in November 2019, I'd worked for *The Northern Echo* group for almost 55 years. Several of those years were spent in a little office – a cubby hole, truth to tell – next to the head office library.

Newspaper libraries weren't like public libraries, chiefly because they didn't have many books or, rather regrettably, fines for the non-return of that which had been "borrowed". Until the miracle advent of electronic storage and retrieval in the late 1980s they were a repository for cuttings and photographic files, both as hard copies but the latter much more comprehensive.

Though the *Echo's* four-storey headquarters in Darlington town centre is now echoing and near-empty – the hope's to sell for a residential and commercial mix and drastically to downsize elsewhere – the top floor library remains, seldom visited by mortals but said nocturnally to be frequented by the restless spirits of newspapermen past, perhaps anxious because the Red Lion's shut.

Unsure of the category into which I fall, I'm back in the office this morning for the first time in two years, the cobwebbed library a reminder of another age – if not cuttings edge, as now almost would be supposed, a treasure house, nonetheless. If only there were still someone to make the coffee (or, come to that, a kettle with which to make it.)

There are other disappointments, the first that in the great ghostly line-up of football team packets there's nothing between Spennymoor United and Stenhousemuir (and precious little on Stenhousemuir, either.) Whither Stanley United?

What of the storms, of the stalwarts, of those wonderful sides from the sixties?

The "news" section initially seems more promising, plump packets – Stanley A-D, E-H and so forth – suggesting rich pickings until the realisation that, yet again, this is the "other" Stanley, the big blinking brother 20 miles to the north, the one which, as a separate packet improbably reminds, used to have an all-happening zoo.

Stanley, Crook – as it's labelled – is much more anorexically archived. Aware of its ongoing identity crisis, I look also for a "Wooley Terrace" packet but can find nothing between Wombleton and World's End (which, cataclysmically, is near Thirsk.) Though Mount Pleasant was on road signs at the entry to the village, the Mount Pleasant packet contains just one titchy two-paragraph cutting and in any case proves to be a hamlet of the same name near Guisborough.

There are little newsworthy nuggets, incorporated elsewhere into the text – a couple of fires, early 70s petitions against the Category D demolition of Wooley Terrace and Stanley Terrace, futile protests later in that decade against closure of the doctors' surgery. The *Echo* somewhat generously supposed Stanley to be "remote" and, yet more fancifully, that villages faced a "near-three mile journey" to the health centre in Crook. They had, of course, to "brave" the cold.

Then suddenly there's a breakthrough, a precious pearl among the dust-dry oysters. It's the story of how Stanley, perhaps uniquely in Britain, was named following a vote at a public meeting.

Confusion had abounded for many years, chiefly because of the

Echoing – the newspaper offices

"other" Stanley – which a later chapter is going to have to visit – but also because, as the first chapter suggested, no one could agree on a place name, anyway. "For years there has been postal chaos," said the *Echo*, inarguably.

Matters weren't helped because even the Wooley Terrace camp was split, some inexplicably opting to add "Post Office" to the address, though Wooley Terrace post office was in any case no longer in Wooley Terrace itself. It was bad enough when parcels were wrongly delivered there, worst yet when a van dropped off a three-piece suite.

At least they had a pillar box. One of Ray Ion's cuttings, October 1911, records the council's concern that despite years of promises nothing of the sort had been provided.

At a public meeting in the Green Hut, called by Crook and Willington Urban District Council on April 28 1965, no fewer than seven possible village names – Stanley, Stanley Crook, Peases Stanley, Wooley, Hill Top Crook, Mount Stanley and Stanley Hill Top were put to the electorate. Windy Ridge had also been proposed – an understatement, the *Echo* reporter thought though, blown out, it failed to make the ballot paper. The chances of the meeting reaching a conclusion were slim, the reporter added. He was wrong.

Robert Marsh, a village school teacher and renowned local cricketer,, told the gathering that the name "Stanley" was found in parish records dating back to 1371. Local councillor and school caretaker Joe Stephenson – the member for Mount Pleasant ward – reckoned that England had five Stanleys and eight Mount Pleasants (or possibly, grammatically, Mounts Pleasant.) Football club president Johnny Hood, 80, spoke in favour of Windy Hill, perhaps remembering that there was a

Windy Nook near Gateshead.

Ethel Armstrong – village shopkeeper, sister of the sitting MP and aunt of a future member – thus underlying the well-known fact that almost everyone in Co Durham had an Aunty Ethel – proposed Stanley Hill Top but appears not to have backed her own horse.

When the motions were put, Stanley Crook received 26 votes, Stanley 11, Wooley five, Peases Stanley two, Hill Top Crook and Mount Stanley two apiece and Stanley Hill Top none whatsoever. When the top two were again put to the vote, Stanley, Crook received 32 votes and Stanley 15.

Attentive readers will have realised that Stanley Hill Top, about as popular as a UK entry in the Eurovision Song Contest, has been the preferred style pretty much throughout the book and is also the heraldic title chosen by Baroness Armstrong. "Stanley Crook" sounds clumsy, the contrivance that it is, a bit like one of those rather dodgy door-to-door brush salesmen from the 1950s. This is our *nul points* moment, but probably it's too late now.

A year after the public vote, the *Echo* checked how things were going. "Even worse than they were before," said village postmaster Bill Wilson. "They'd have been better off just calling it Wooley."

15: cross purposes

August 28 2021

Just 200 yards from the North East Moto-X Club's big meeting, day one of three, it's so improbably quiet that I'm convinced I must have got the dates mixed up. The only audible drone is from the bees, and even they sound like they could use a Horlicks and an early night. Baffling.

They race 14 days a year at Wooley Grange, once the site of Stanley's biggest pit, more dust than a 3ft seam but probably much less deleterious to health and safety (unless, of course, the riders go A-over-T across the handlebars, a not uncommon occurrence.)

Wooley Grange may also have been the site of a rabbit coursing handicap, reported in *The Northern Echo* in October 1881 at which Plunger beat Jack Shepherd. Mr T Iveson was pistol firer and Mr John Parkin referee. If they still have rabbit coursing up that way, they shouldn't.

It's a splendidly sunny Saturday afternoon. A few decades ago they'd have been playing village football and cricket, perhaps simultaneously, just across the fields. Now there's not so much as an illicit game of three card brag or even kids in that wonderfully equipped playpark. I've never yet seen a soul in Stanley playpark.

Though almost silently – pretty quietly, anyway – the MX folk are indeed encamped, a sign by the entrance advising that despite all their best efforts, motor sport can be dangerous. Though somewhat self-evident, it's doubtless legally recommended. Another sign warns of hazardous chemicals; it was never like this at the Little House on the Prairie, save for brolly waving women, anyway.

I ask a chap in a high-viz the whereabouts of Anthony Wright, the organiser. "Dunno," he says, off-handedly, "but if you find him, tell the bugger I want to see him, an' all."

At once it's evident that this is a family occasion and that many are intent on making an August bank holiday of it. Though boys and girls must be six before allowed to participate, some seem so little that they might have nappies beneath their leathers and stabilisers supporting their 50cc bikes.

A vehicle has the registration MX10VAN, the plate perhaps worth more than the bikes within. A bike carries the number 666. Mark of the devil, isn't it?

On such an afternoon, the attendant Mister Softee has no need of the hard sell – how might Wooley miners' lives have been different had Mr Softee and not the White City awaited the end of the fore shift? There's also a confectionery van, a fish

Big wheel – Anthony Smith

and chip van, a couple of bouncy castles and something which looks like a ghost train but may be more substantial.

Big Mick's Street Food is owned by Anthony Wright, aforesaid. "It should really be Big Anth's," he concedes, inarguably, though the depiction on the side of the trailer bears a passing resemblance, nonetheless. A row of temporary toilets prompts the idle thought (and probably the obvious answer) of what the colliers did when similarly caught short.

Big Anth says that he lives in Stanley. We spend several minutes discussing the community's life and times until it becomes obvious that he, too, means the former West Stanley, the ineluctable big brother. It seems almost treacherous.

I'm so preoccupied in watching out for wayward motor bikes that I trip over a tent peg and damn near break a leg.

MX enthusiasts have been revving up on this site for 27 years, since land owner William Marley wanted somewhere for his son to practise and decreed that others might muck in. Anth, 42, has been involved for 22 years. "It's a good local track and a brilliant farmer," he says, adding that it's the surrounding trees to the south and west which pretty much ensure that Stanley stays not just out of sight but out of earshot, too.

Roar deal, he insists that they work closely with the council and the neighbours. "We get on well, we keep them informed of our timetable but they hardly know we're here. There've been very few complaints. It's a great sport, an addictive sport. It gives the kids something to do, off the streets and out of trouble, and it gives them a perspective in life."

To the east, the view's predictably magnificent. Those optically equipped might not just view Saltburn, as they can from the bedroom windows at the Foresters, but with a bit of imagination Scarborough, as well.

It's still so comparatively quiet that it's possible to overhear snatches of conversation about clutches and camrods and things though not, of course, to understand a single supercharged syllable.

Anth's had a problem, however – the paramedics have failed to show up, meaning that only practice laps are permitted. The bikes quite literally take off, even so. Forget the No 1 bus, these guys are the real Stanley flyers.

Though assiduously watered, the track's as dry as a Hill Top pub crawl. The fence seems a bit shoogly, as the clansmen would have it, but none ventures beyond it. Inexplicably, a chap's sheltering beneath a very large umbrella. A youngster comes off at a bend, pretty much says "Bother" and "Oh blow" – see under *Wind in the Willows* - and gets back on the horse. "It can still be a dangerous sport," says Anth. "A lad of 15 has been killed in Scotland only today."

As if to underline the point, the club website warns that fireworks are strictly not allowed and that transgressors will be barred. "I don't care who you are," it adds in very large type.

The oldest competitor is 78-year-old Dave Beck – Dave Beck Senior – joined by his son and granddaughter. Some young lads are stripped to the waist, leather boots and leather pants, rather resembling some of those American all-in wrestlers though usually much less corpulent.

I leave after a couple of hours. Not 100 yards away the farmer has been making hay, just like the MX family on a sunny Stanley afternoon.

The next appointment isn't until 4pm. On yet anther dander around the village I come across Frank Cowans, seated with his wife Ina in his 84-year-old Austin 12/4 Ascot, a vehicle much cherished. They're talking in the sunshine to Harry Hodgson, an old friend, who lives barely 50 yards from where the Little House once served the Northern League's finest provender and remembers very well the night that someone set it alight.

"The lights at home kept flickering. We went outside to see what was wrong and it was blazing like billy-o. There was no water up here, the fire brigade had to fetch it from the school."

Harry moved to Stanley 40 years ago from Gainford, in Teesdale, indicates the handsome trees which line the road. "Not waist high when we came here," he says.

Long runner – Frank and Ina Cowans,
with Harry Hodgson (right)

Frank was for 44 years a travelling butcher serving the village. Conversation again turns to local shops – "two Co-ops, two fish shops, Frank Hogan's, Ethel Armstrong's, post office" – today's top estimate around 20. Though they themselves live a few miles away in Willington, both Frank and Ina's daughters – Francis Street and Chapel Street – are on the Hill Top. "They absolutely love it," says Frank. It will prove a good day for buffing Stanley's image.

It's still just 3 45pm. I requisition a bench by the Windy Ridge war memorial, absorb the glorious views southwards and attempt what the continentals might appropriately suppose a few *aides memoire.*

The reverie's soon interrupted by a chap who's puffed up Billy Row Bank, nowhere near as breathlessly as my own ascent a few hours earlier. who offers the time of day and wonders if I'm Mike. This is Paul French, the 4pm appointment, the West Hammer who left the South of France for the North-East of England. "I'd been all over Europe but never further north than Blackpool," says Paul, now 58.. "I absolutely love Stanley." Probably there'll need to be a chapter heading ere long. *The French connection* seems pretty much inescapable.

Shirt sleeved, he warms to his theme. "Down south they know nothing about this area. Co Durham must be the best kept secret in the world." So what did he know about the North-East? "Alan Shearer, Newcastle United, the Vikings," he says. "That's about it."

Their home, part of a former chateau, was in south-western France near Bordeaux. Only the Riviera has a higher average temperature. Had no one told him that Stanley might be a degree or two cooler, a bit on the fresh side? "In France every day was like this," he says. "It could get a bit too hot, a bit oppressive at times. I love the seasons, anyway."

Chief difference between a Stanley winter and a southern French winter? "Longer," says Paul, at once. Their first year at 53 Mount Pleasant, 2019-20, they'd run the heating from October to mid-May. "It seemed a bit much but I also installed a log burner. We got through quite a lot of logs."

Narinda, his wife – Narin, for short – is Indian. With little risk of contradiction, he supposes her the only Indian in the village. "There was a bit of snow, but it was all right," says Paul. The Hill Top may be lulling him into a sense of false security.

He and Narin, she seven years younger – "I met her that when she was 13 and I was working 12 hours shifts in the factory" – were both managers in the optical industry. He's now retired ("I had three good pensions") she works for Specsavers in Durham.

They bought their house in France for around £108,000 in 2011 – "about as big as those houses over there," says Paul, pointing collectively to six or seven Mount Pleasant dwellings behind us. "It was never going to work; we were always going to run out of money and we did, and then good old Brexit came along. If we'd stayed we'd have had to take on the system, which can get very complicated. I also started to worry about living in France when I was 70. A lot of people seem to last about ten years and then want to come home again."

They still own the house in France, though hope to sell it soon. "When we came back we just wanted somewhere cheap as chips. Like everyone else, I'd probably live in Cornwall if I had the money, but I hadn't."

They looked at properties in Norfolk and in Grimsby then took a room at the North Point hotel in Tow Law and had a look around the North-East – including the quaintly named No Place, a village – here we go again – near that other Stanley of overwhelming presence. They looked at a house in Willington, didn't like the area – "too many burned out cars" – decided against Tow Law itself.

En passant, almost, they noticed the Mount Pleasant house but were told by the agent that there was no one to show them round. "I'd never heard anything like it in my life," says Paul. "The sellers wouldn't have been very happy if they'd known. We'd seen photographs of the inside but the first time I stepped foot inside it was turning the key after we'd bought it."

The end terrace house cost £58,000 – "a bit more than our budget" – but Mount Pleasant lived greatly up to its name. despite the prevailing winds. "At first I wondered why there were so few flowers in the little front gardens, but they I realised they could be blown at 45 degrees. It's still like that out the back."

If there's a downside, he supposes, it's the absence of shops and licensed premises – "it's the convenience, in London everything's 24/7 these days". The upside's the friendliness. "The welcome's been fantastic. In London everyone walks round with their heads down, no eye contact. When we lived in Basingstoke, I didn't even know the neighbours' names. It's so informal here, and the neighbours are lovely."

That there seems something of a social vacuum may be, he supposes, because newcomers don't seem to stay long. In Wooley Meadows, just behind his house, he reckons every house has been on the market in the last two years. "They buy houses relatively cheaply but still mortgaged to the hilt They make a few bob and then move on. There's not really time to become involved with anything."

In time, he supposes, he and Narin will also be on the move – not emigrating back to the south but flitting up to Weardale, which they find yet more attractive. In the meantime they're trying to persuade other friends in the south to follow their example. "They just don't know what they're missing," says Paul. "That's what friends are for."

Though our bench is squarely in Stanley, Billy Row workmen's club is barely 100 yards down the hill. Paul's never been inside nor, for that matter, drunk Newcastle Brown Ale. Formalities over, I introduce him to both.

In the bar the lads with no great enthusiasm are watching Newcastle United, on a table in the back room some slightly second-best leeks are laid on a trestle table. The labels proclaim them exhibits in Nicky's Leek Club, Nicky's being the local name for the Miners Arms – Billy Nicholson, long-licensed to sell ales, wines and spirits – a few yards further down. Though it closed many years ago, the leeks live on.

Trevor Smith – encountered back in May on a bad day for Sunderland – is again hospitable, says we'd be surprised at how many folk around that way now have southern accents. "We welcome them all, good lads – most of them anyway," he adds.

Trevor also reveals that it's the club's own leek show, that great tradition of North-East mining communities, the following Friday evening. The No 1 bus timetable must be scrutinised once again.

16: leek pudding

September 3 2021

Three others alight the bus outside Billy Row Club, and with but one purpose. There must be at least 25 in, of whom two are female and one is playing darts against himself. He appears to be losing. A big night then, though all things (of course) are comparative.

Back in the day, they recall, the leek, flower and vegetable show awards evening would be preceded at 4pm by a three-course hot meal for 240 and followed by entertainment. "Real good turns, Bobby Thompson and people like that," says Alan Brown.

Those without green fingers were allowed in about six o'clock. "Mind," adds Alan, "there wasn't an awful lot of room left after all that."

In its happy heyday, plots thickening and leeks burgeoning, there might have been 100 entries. Tonight there are 19, some from the same garden. "So long as you were a member of the workmen's club, it didn't matter where you grew them," says Alan. "We had entries from Frosterley and all over.

"It's what the miners did. If you were down the pit all day or all night, you'd want to be out in the garden with your leeks or in the fresh air with your pigeons. It's an age thing, there's not the commitment now."

For the green-fingered, even for the cack-handed, rewards were huge. Clubs throughout the North-East would annual-ly welcome pantechnicons from the local department store – Doggart's more often than not – overflowing with prizes from three-piece suites to washing machines. For 20th place, it's re-

Show time – back in 2000

called, the entrant might only get a fridge.

Doggart's, once Bishop Auckland-based but with branches across the area, features prominently in Co Durham folklore. In the 50s and 60s, it's widely claimed, impoverished supporters of Bishop Auckland and Crook Town football clubs would take out a Doggart's club, sell it on at a reduced price and in a twist on the old principle of buy-now-pay-later fund another weekend at Wembley.

At Billy Row, it's said, the club would hire a bus so that those dissatisfied with their prizes could return them to the shop in Sunderland to exchange for something of equal value but greater appeal. One or two pit stops on the way back made the day out second only to the club trip and in Sunderland they didn't have to worry about crabs.

"It wasn't just the prizes which were important," says Alan. "There was a real excitement about the occasion, the club was the centre of things. The big thing for your 18th birthday wasn't the party, it was getting out your club cards. If you won Billy Row Club leek show, you were talk of the village for months."

It's a warm night inside and out, a night both clubbable and companionable, a reminder of former times save that if the lads want a Woodbine, they needs must inhale out the front.

Alan Brown, now 73 and born and raised in Billy Row, is secretary/treasurer of the leek club and chairman/treasurer of the pigeon club, its wings yet more inexorably clipped by time. These days there are just five members, one of them up from Crook since the town's workmen's club permanently pulled down the shutters.

Affable and helpful, he sits tonight like St Matthew at the re-

ceipt of custom, a little plastic pease pudding pot overflowing with notes of the realm – letter draw, Tote, raffle, subs. None pays by credit card. Of his own leeks, and of those entered in his wife's name – "I grow them, of course" – Alan is greatly pessimistic. "They've just gone to seed, expired, passed their sell-by date," he says. "You have to enter but I'll be last, disqualified. It's been a bad year for quite a few. I mean, what do you do?"

His mementoes include a photograph of his dad when club champion in 1973, another of the concert room wall-to-wall with entries and a copy of the schedule from as recently as the year 2000 – 23 different flower and vegetable classes, entry 20p a go, top prizes £7 for the winner but mostly £4. Most entries became the property of the club and were sold at auction, but the champions could hang on to their leeks.

Upstairs in the semi-abandoned games room, tonight's leeks

Flagging? Alan Brown

are benched on a board covering the single snooker table. A carrier bag bears the slogan "That's all folks" but not, it's to be hoped, prophetically. Bobby Latcham, the judge, has completed his tasks – "doing the cards," they call it – indicates a pair of leeks which would have been best in show had they been properly washed and presented. "Ten minutes work," sighs Alan.

Each pair of leeks is adorned with their position in the show and with a little tick-off sticker, advising the extent of their growing pains, the error of their ways. "Soft decaying leek", perhaps, "bent leek", "blanched leek" or even "general appearance and uniformity." "Those have too big leaves, they're all wrong," says Bobby, pointing towards a sort of growers' naughty stool.

"Them's mine," says Alan, gloomily.

The winner, 112 cubic inches, is Barry Moore, his father also a past Billy Row champion. "It's a bit embarrassing winning with leeks like these," he says. "My mother and father grew a lot better than this."

Barry, bless him, then becomes emotional. Earlier in the year he'd spent a month in hospital with Covid, during which period both his parents died. It's a reminder of how things are still fixed and that it may yet be a very long time before everything in the garden's rosy.

Leeks appear to be measured in different ways, some in cubic inches and others weighed, though there seems little doubt that in former times 112 cubic inches might scarcely have filled grandma's broth pan. The better news is that the biggest and best all appear to have North-East roots.

Guinness World Records reckons the biggest to have been the 23lb 9oz monster grown in 2018 by Paul Rochester from Sea-

ham and exhibited at the Canna UK National Giant Vegetable Championships in Malvern, Worcestershire – four ounces heavier than his previous global giant.

Paul reckoned the secret of his success partly to be that he played Glenn Miller to his prize crop, presumably to get them in the mood. Whether Billy Row's best are similarly serenaded is sadly not recorded, but they probably prefer brass bands.

Another record, 572 cubic inches and improbably said to be the same size as the engine of a Ford Ka, was claimed by Northumberland pensioner Geoff Moscrop at the John Smith's Leek and

Digging deep – Barry Moore

Onion Show in Blyth, his leeks so perennially gargantuan that he'd had to adopt a set of suitcase scales in order accurately to weigh them. He probably didn't have any Glenn Miller CDs but talked of a "gut feeling", the phrase perhaps unfortunate, about how often the leeks should be watered.

Old pitmen, it's whispered, would have similar gut feelings but not always from a watering can and rarely with such successful results.

Around Stanley and Billy Row they also still talk of Joey Jones, a railway signalman from Stanhope, in Weardale, twice world champion in the 1980s. "Lovely feller, great character," says Alan. "His brother George was just as successful with the pigeons."

The internet also digs up another world record claim, 20lb 5oz, by John Pearson from Sunderland – the accompanying photograph with his prize specimens suggesting that he might almost have challenged them to two falls, two submissions or a knock-out. "Anyone can grow leeks like this so long as they have the right pips," John had said, modestly.

The same show had recorded a 107lb marrow, a 54lb cabbage and a 16lb 4 oz onion, enough to bring tears to the eyes. However briefly, the headline on the internet report also suggested a remarkable coincidence. The contest had taken place in Stanley. Perhaps commensurately in the circumstances, it was that blooming big brother once again.

We're back in the bar downstairs: no turns, no treacle tart, no triumph and no three-piece Dralon with which to beautify the front room and mollify the Mrs. "Apart from the first three they all get the same money," says Alan. "The first maybe gets £35

more."

Tommy Todd, pigeon club chairman and now the last high-flyer in Stanley, lives way up on the Heights of Alma. Inevitably but almost reluctantly, conversation's again turned to how greatly things have changed.

"Massively," says Tommy, on the Hill Top since 1955 save for a few years on loan to Tow Law. "The leek show was the best house of the year, when you walked in the concert room with leeks, flowers and vegetables benched around every wall the sight and the smell almost took your breath away."

It was very competitive, he adds, no leek slashing but evident trench warfare, nonetheless. Now there's peace in these times. "Everyone wanted to win it, " says Tommy. "These days it's more social than competitive."

Back then, he adds, pretty much everyone knew everyone else. "There's 70 new houses below me on the Heights of Alma and most of them are strangers. I maybe know three of them. They're missing a good night here."

The last bus leaves from across the road, shortly before 9pm. As I wait, again admiring the vast nocturnal vista, one of the Willie Woodbine boys shouts across to enquire if it's been a good night.

"It's been great," I say and so, nostalgically, it has.

17: the other man's grass

September 15 2021

Wasn't it the American folkie Roger Miller, erstwhile King of the Road, who in the mid-60s sang that England Swings (like a pendulum do)? Times and language change, and not always for the better.

England Swings becomes a buzzing, irksome earworm as today I circle, ever decreasing, around Stanley – not for once the Hill Top, but the former West Stanley in north-west Durham, the blooming big brother. As they used to say on O-level English papers, it's a compare and contrast exercise, a little interlude, a chance to see how the other half lives.

Wikipedia's quite chatty on the subject, recording not just that the urban Stanley had a population of around 31,000 in 2019 – about 30,000 more than the folk who live on the hill – but that in 1999 a Stanley takeaway owner called Haresh Ramadan changed its name to Harry Ramadan's. Harry Ramsden's famed fish shop chain began legal action, poor Haresh backed down and sold up two years later.

The best story, however, concerns the time around 2007 that the former Kings Head pub was transformed into the Local Spa Hotel, said to be a fully equipped swingers' club – "one of the most popular swingers' clubs in the North of the UK" says Wiki – with fully equipped play rooms, dungeon and "greedy girl" nights. There were letting rooms, too, so that – as the promoters put it – when the club shuts the fun needn't stop.

Whatever all that was about, it probably wasn't what Roger Miller had in mind, nor the sort of swinging that went on in Shildon Rec.

There'd been 500 objections, the *Evening Chronicle* reporting in 2013 that the goings-on had sparked outrage. "Sparked outrage" is one of those journalistic phrases, like "rookie cop" and "set to descend", which none in real life ever employs but which the inky trade supposes on-message. What particularly seemed to concern the *Chronicle* was that there was a chip shop just two doors down and that the two queues might be confused, cross-contaminated even, though it was unclear which was deemed to be in the greater moral danger.

There'd also been sightings of "tarts and vicars", though whether authentic gentlemen of the cloth or impious impersonators was not recorded. Same goes for the tarts. Visitors had been seen to carry plastic bags, it was said, though probably not from Waitrose and for a purpose which may only be imagined.

In 2018 the *Chronicle* was again on the case, reporting that police had "swooped" – flying squad, perhaps, or maybe just rookie cops – after a report that a child had been seen entering the premises. When it proved to be a rather undersized female adult they left – of course – "red faced." The club was said to have a fully equipped dungeon with a "mistress" but to be consensual, wholly within the law and to offer jobs for seven people, all shapes and sizes, in an unemployment blackspot.

It was Stanley's most improbable development since the aforementioned zoo, around 1970, though there, of course, whip-cracking comparisons should probably end. Besides, though its denizens may have found a thick skin to be of benefit, the swingers' club didn't have an elephant.

Perhaps because of the understandable desire for discretion, further on-line research has not been enlightening. An attempt to access what appears to be the website is met with the interesting message that "you do not have the necessary permission for the specified page to perform the requested action."

So near so Spa, as they used to say in a different context. Swings and roundabouts, does the place even still exist? One thing's certain – it would never happen on the Hill Top.

T'other , bigger Stanley's accessed by the 16 or 16A Go North East bus, what they call the Durham Diamond, every 15 minutes from the city centre. It makes a change, anyway. The name's probably a nod to the Black Diamond – or was it the Blue? – the privately owned company which in former times covered the route. "The bus that's as posh as your house," it says on the back, though it's to be hoped it's a bit posher than that. I'm hoping to include a later chapter on buses up and over the Hill Top, too.

Just this morning, a piece in the paper had warned that a number of Go North East services wouldn't be operating because of a Covid-related driver shortage and asking that passengers refrain from taking out their "ill feeling" on the poor drivers who remained. "Useless bastards," says a chap with a southern accent, possibly illiterate, boarding ahead of me.

Linguists will understand that the southern accent is divined from the way that he pronounces the b-word, rather as in barmpot.

The bus journey's enhanced by the automaton, well-spoken lass, who announces every stop. The Stanley area includes well-researched villages like Quaking Houses and (once again) No Place, like Tantobie, Catchgate and, perhaps most improbably of all, Blomfontein. How did that get there, for heaven's sake? The bus station's impressive – solar powered, thought-

fully designed, clearly signed and well kept. The problem's upon leaving it: how do you ask a stranger, much less a female stranger, directions to the neighbourhood swingers' club?

Nor does it help that in terms of what the inky trade likes to call investigative journalism I was always Watson to someone else's Holmes – possibly even Mrs Hudson who, it will be recalled, kept the Great Detective in coffee and cocaine.

Is it a clue that the e-cig shop is called the Vaping Dungeon, that the travel agency offers "adult only" trips to the Caribbean – Jamaica? No, go as you please – and that there's a place called Sexy Nails, which is probably just cosmetic but could indicate some particularly extreme form of sado-masochism?

Stanley swings?

Cautiously asked the whereabouts of the Spa Hotel, a chap on a bench essays a failure to understand the Queen's English and hurries away, a taxi driver attempts to do better but proves unable to tell right from left, which may be seriously disadvantageous in the hackney cab business. An elderly gentleman near Oxhill at last remembers the Spa – "mind, they knocked it doon just after the war," he says, adding perhaps unnecessarily that he was only a bairn back then.

Just when the tom-toms are almost becoming audible, when reports might be starting to circulate that potentially the oldest swinger in town has asked the vicar's wife the way to the swingers' club – the apostrophe apposite, assuming that it takes two – I stumble across it, an unprepossessing place on a street corner with no sign of life save for a dog barking anxiously within.

Sherlock Holmes had a famous case of the dog barking – or, rather, not barking – in the night but this was still just dinner time.

The name Spa Hotel remains above the door. A board outside offers sauna, steam rooms and hot tub but no sign of scampi and chips. With no obvious connection, other hoardings promote 99p Big Macs and the services of Specsavers. A small notice in the window advises that it's illegal to smoke on the premises – everything else legit, then? – while another registers their membership of the FSB.

Financial Services Bureau? Funny Sexual Behaviour? Federation of Small Businesses it, rather disappointingly, transpires.

Triumphant nonetheless, I head back up the main street, order a Brown Ale in the Top House, its bar crepuscular and slightly crestfallen, and settle in the corner for some good old-fashioned eavesdropping. A chap of about 60 is telling his mate that after 12 years he still really misses their lass, not least – rather curiously – because she was a good freezer filler. It's only when he recalls the difficult decision to have her euthanised – and that her name was Digger – that I guess (and rather hope) that he's talking about the dog.

The returning Diamond has to decant on the outskirts of Durham because of a big fire in the city centre, leaving a mile-and-a-half mile walk to the railway station. Happily for Go North East, I've no ill-feelings whatsoever.

On the Hill Top, so far as reasonably may be ascertained, the only swingers – and they but infrequently – are those in the Jobson Meadows playground. How else might the two Stanleys, *magna* and *parva* as the Romans might have had it, compare and contrast?

Both were once heavily dependent on coal, both have seen significant commercial decline, both have old and new cheek by jowl – in north Durham from Loud Terrace to Broadwood Mews. The larger Stanley, if only because of size and number, may have greater opportunity for community involvement; its smaller cousin has views which are just incomparable. Both offer house prices to make a southerner's eyes pop.

Old habit, I ring home to report that the Diamond has delivered but wonder aloud what might be done next. "You'll have to be like the Lambton Worm" says Sharon – a reference, it may be recalled, to the queer beast that roamed about picking up bits of news until young Lambton improbably mistook it for a salmon.

Wiki says that the name's Old English *staenig-lean*, meaning stony clearing, and that former West Stanley residents have included Hillary Clinton's grandfather, Kevin Keegan's grandfather – a hero of the 1909 Burns Pit disaster which killed 160 men – the actor Alun Armstrong and one of the blokes behind the Muppets.

Perhaps with confusion elsewhere in mind, the Wikipedia page is also quick to point out that Stanley should not be confused with East Stanley. That's in the Falkland Islands, it adds. The Hill Top doesn't get a mention.

There's an estate agency near the bus station, outside which a gentleman assiduously sweeps their bit of pavement. Inevitably I'm reminded of Nora Batty, sans stockings. A detached three bedroom house is on offer at £128,000, a two-bed terraced property ("renovation opportunity") a snip at £42,000.

Big brother, the other Stanley

Elsewhere, a four bedroom "town house" is £145,000 and a two bedroom semi £84,995.

Footfall in the pedestrianised front street is light, football in the circumstances quite possible. Many shops are shuttered. They don't still do Wednesday half-day, do they? The Royal appears to have abdicated, Royal Road to have had the red carpet pulled from beneath its feet. Store Twenty One seems to have been unlucky for some, the telephone shop not to be taking calls, the Ginger Giraffe Gift Shop to have failed to keep on giving. Long abandoned, the Tantobie Board School (1891) is an egregious eyesore.

The *Stanley News* office no longer goes to press, either. Its former reporters include Yvonne Ridley, captured by the Taliban when working for the *Express* in the Middle East and so taken with their way of life that she converted to Islam. She now runs a community newspaper, has an honorary PhD from a Swiss university and writes books in the Scottish borders.

The town has two banks, though – two more than there are in Shildon – a veritable hirsuteness of barbers, only one called Cut Above, and a preening parade of what once might have been called beauty parlours but these days seem to favour the term aesthetics. A tanning saloon has a notice "New tubes fitted", but I had that fairly miraculously done at the James Cook Hospital in Middlesbrough a couple of years ago and feel no need to darken their door. The ear and nose waxing is, apparently, just for the blokes and though it may not be available on the NHS it has to be said that they're welcome.

That the Stanley urban area has Slimming World classes in different venues six evenings a week may further indicate eagerness for what might be supposed a new look. The town council's website suggests that it, too, is keen on beautification – "the streets in and around Stanley are erupting in colour" it says, though that may have been a little earlier in the year.

A shop called Purple Dragon, sub-titled House of Incense, offers "unique gifts" and no matter that half of them appear to be tea pots. No kettles. Another business is simply called MCM Advice. I'm tempted to ask them where on earth a decent pub might be found in Stanley, but decide that that might be too difficult.

There are a great many white taxis but, seemingly, not a great many fares. It may be what comes of the right hand not knowing what the left is doing. Over the road the Civic Centre doubles as a cinema, Tom and Jerry on Tuesdays, and is advertising a pantomime, Beauty and the Beast, from December 15-24. It doesn't say who's in it. A little crocodile of well-mannered school kids heads for a swimming lesson at the adjacent Louisa Centre.

A few doors along from the Empire Club and Institute, the Imperial advertises cask and craft beers and "great food" served every day. Without a break in her gum chewing, the barmaid advises that they haven't any real ale. It seems prudent not to ask about the great food, lest that be confined to chewing gum (one careless owner.)

The sun's still shining as I head back on the ever-so-posh 16A. Who knows, I may have to swing by here again.

18: Facebook lovers

September 23 2021

Karl Utley was born in Halifax and spent his early years in those parts. Andrea, his wife, was born and bred on the Hill Top – "Windy City" as she likes to call it – but it's the West Yorkshireman, whatever the wind speed, who most vigorously flies the flag for Stanley.

Successful in the furniture business, he spends much of his spare time helping curate the *If You Lived in Stanley, Billy Row and Surrounding Areas* Facebook page and researching some of its content.

"It's absolutely fascinating what you can come up with," says Karl. "I don't sleep very well and sometimes I can be sitting at my Mac at two o'clock in the morning, make a really exciting discovery and feel the need to share it with Andrea."

"It's so annoying," says Andrea, wholly affectionately.

"Enthralling," says her husband.

"Boring," she corrects.

Clearly they are happy to differ, but if put to the casting vote – well, sagacious readers must judge for themselves.

Karl started the Stanley page about nine years ago – "there'd been a bit of a spat with the Billy Row page" he says. Soon afterwards there was an old friends' gathering, Stanley Reunited – "70 or 80 people turned up, fabulous night". Though originally intended as a winged chariot for nostalgia – a theme he zealously and sometimes macabrely perpetuates, as shortly we shall hear – the page's range is now more that of the scattergun.

Content in the days before our meeting has ranged from free potatoes (an offer enthusiastically accepted) to an on-line enquiry about whether the ice cream man's in the vicinity, from a request not to feed the horses to an appeal over the entomological identity of a caterpillar found in someone's garden.

Another thread wonders if the Hound of the Baskervilles has been let loose in Stanley Crook (a second reference in about three pages to Sherlock Holmes.). "It's been howling all day," it adds. Any amount have lost stuff, and found a home on Facebook.

Its being the Hill Top, there's almost inevitably a flurry of snow and reminders of the winter of 1947, particular reference to the absence back then of central heating and of what might be termed internal sanitation. "Folk had to get out of bed in the freezing cold and dig 50 yards through the snow to get coal for the fire," says one post, perhaps discreetly avoiding reference to how they tackled the other problem. Perhaps they could work it out for themselves.

Karl had also recorded that on September 7 this year Stanley, unknown to all but himself, had had a royal visitor – or at least the Queen's helicopter flying directly overhead *en route* to Balmoral. How did he know? "I have this app, I have lots of apps, which tracks the helicopter's flights. I was at work, heard a big helicopter overhead and was amazed to find what it was."

Whether Her Majesty waved to the patriotic Hill Toppers below, or indeed essayed a royal salute, is sadly not recorded, though her parents certainly had – and at rather closer quarters.

It was February 1939, King George VI and Queen Elizabeth on a three-day visit to the depressed North-East that had started with the launch of a warship, *King George V*, on the Tyne, continued with a visit to Durham and then off past Oakenshaw and through Stanley and Sunniside to open a "social services centre" in Tow Law top which an earlier chapter referred.

At Oakenshaw, the entourage – hood down on the royal Daimler Landauette – had been greeted by miners "with grime on their faces and clad in mining garb" while others in the workshops clanged their hammers. On the Hill Top hundreds lined Mount Pleasant and Francis Street and at Tow Law it started to snow. As might not in the circumstances be supposed, there's nothing new under the sun.

Now 45, Karl was nine or ten years old when his parents, Bill and Ann, became steward and stewardess of Billy Row Workmen's. Before that they'd spent a couple of years at Meadowfield British Legion Club, south of Durham. "Billy Row head-hunted them," he says. "My first impression of the area was that everyone was very friendly, but maybe they just wanted to keep in with my dad."

He recalls sitting in the club lounge to watch the 1986 World Cup final, one of many occasions on which that big building overflowed. "Sunday nights were 50-50 dancing and bingo, Tuesdays more dancing, Saturdays they'd be queuing out of the door to get into the concert room. On top of that there were all the pigeon men, and leek club lads, in the bar."

Andrea recalls a big playground roundabout and a slide, yet bigger. "Too big," she says, "I once fell off and badly cut my leg."

Then there was the fabled club trip, the annual exodus to Ely-

sium. "In 1986 it went to Whitley Bay, nine or ten buses and the Tall Ships off the coast, but there was talk of when there'd be 30 or 40 buses, lined up from one end of Mount Pleasant to the other."

Karl spent 18 months at Peases West primary school, just down the hill, before transferring to Wolsingham Comp. Though the club was in Billy Row, by as much as 50 yards, he recalls hanging out around Stanley and with Stanley lads. "A lady called Doris Sowerby ran a youth club in the village hall, I think there's a plaque to her, and there was a scout group, too.

"I don't think there was any rivalry between Billy Row lads and Stanley lads, though there might have been a bit between Billy Row and Stanley on one hand and Tow Law and Esh Winning on the other."

With mates Chris Dakers, John Nelson and Leo Maughan – in those parts pronounced "Maffen" he accurately recalls – they also bought guitars and formed a band called Forever Friends. "We were absolute shite, didn't even have a drummer," says Karl. "All we seemed to do was play Deep Purple and only about two of their tunes at that."

He gained a photography qualification at a college in Middlesbrough, had promotional work accepted by Christian Dior, opened a record shop – McCoy's – in Crook before, what goes around comes around, going into sales. "Educational equipment and stuff, I did pretty well." His furniture company Oak World, employing around 45 staff and operating on-line, is based in Willington.

As kids they'd also played around what Stanley natives call the Bomb Hole, behind Francis Street. It's not a bomb hole at all but a disused quarry, though we'd earlier recalled when a jettisoned bomb had fallen behind Arthur Terrace – "legend has it that a cow was killed," says Karl.

Much more tragically, Wellington bomber DV841, smoke bil-lowing from its tail, had flown low over St Thomas's church on the evening of May 21 1942 and then crashed onto a farmer's field a mile down the hill in Roddymoor. Before rescuers could reach it, the aircraft exploded, killing all five crew – two Australians and three Canadians – on a training flight from RAF

On parade – but why?

Kinningley, near Doncaster. A new plane, it was said to have had fewer than 15 hours flying time.

The dead men were laid in the farmer's cow byre, buried side by side five days later in the West Cemetery in Darlington Already a memorial existed in the North East Aviation museum near Washington; another was unveiled in Crook Community Centre in 2017. A lone piper played a lament for the crew of DV841.

The killing of Billy Spence is said to have caused "great consternation" in Stanley, as well it might have done, Well over a century later, recollection of that dark night still provokes on-line suggestions that sleeping dogs be left to their slumbers.

Karl had been surprised at the mixed reaction after researching the case for the Facebook page. "We think we live in an unruly world now but it was no different all those years ago" he says. "In truth it sounds a little bit like the Wild West."

Burrowing legitimately in the night, he has also found details of an alleged murder at Billy Row 100 years ago and of a burglary, August 1895, at the Foresters Arms in Stanley during the course of which David Swinbank, described as a watchmaker from Ferryhill who'd had several spells of penal servitude, was found in the cellar in "an utterly helpless state of drunkenness" – unsynchronised, it might be supposed - with a pair of pincers and a screwdriver in his pockets and an empty whisky barrel in suspiciously close proximity.

"A singular case" said *The Northern Echo* headline, the papers eager to put an interpretation upon events that these days would have their editors locked up for contempt. "A case of alleged burglary, heard at Auckland on Monday, clearly showed that when a burglar goes burgling it is prudent to act on teetotal principles" the report began.

The wretched Swinbank had been committed for sentence to the Assizes, though Karl has been unable to find out what happened next. "When cases get to the Assizes the trail seems to go cold," he says, though there was a report of the trial of Billy Row miner Alfred Bagnall, charged in 1920 with his wife's murder – the instrument of her demise allegedly having been a poker.

The court heard that not only had the dead woman been "carrying on" with a chap from Willington but, yet more perfidiously, there had been "improper relations". Bagnall claimed that her injuries were effectively, if accidentally, self-inflicted and was acquitted. "A large crowd waited outside the court," said the *Echo*, "and cheered the accused as he left the building."

Then there was the case – "made every newspaper in the land" says Karl – of the eight-year-old from Stanley who accidentally shot and killed his sister. He hasn't yet decided if he wants to run that one.

Billy Spence was a 21-year-old miner whose home at 16 Mount Pleasant was shared with his mother, stepfather and two siblings – one of them his sister Eleanor, known as Nelly. Spence, it was said, was in the habit of "correcting" his sisters – the term "thrashing" was also used, lest any suppose he was merely offering fraternal advice on the proper use of the apostrophe – because his mother was often unwell and his father, for whatever reason, useless.

Late one Sunday evening he'd come home and gone to bed but, woken by noise below, came down to remonstrate – or to give sister Emma a good hiding for her "saucy" response. Nelly, just 18, found herself in possession of a "gully" – used for making garters, it was said – and Billy, accidentally it was claimed, was stabbed.

His mother had "asked him where he was bad" – as in those parts they still do – seemingly thought little of it but made him some "composition tea." Whatever composition tea may have been, it proved not to be efficacious. At 3am the doctor from Crook was sent for and stitched up the wound but, things clearly having taken a turn for the worse, poor Billy died the following evening.

Soon the papers heard of it, and with accustomed disregard for what these days would be called the judicial process. They became quite excitable. "Terrible tragedy at Crook, a man stabbed by his sister" said the *Echo's* Wednesday morning headline with little regard to the concept of innocent until proved guilty. The story added that the "death blow" had been in the vicinity of the bowels.

A toe in unaccustomed waters, even the *Shields Gazette* became involved. "Spence did not complain at the time (of the stabbing) but went out" it averred.

The inquest was held on the Thursday of the same week, Mr Coroner Proud – presumably one of the famed sportsman/solicitors from Bishop Auckland – travelling up to Stanley for the purpose. These days it would be held at an improbable and quite possibly inaccessible venue about two years later.

Back in 1910, to be precise at 5 49 on the morning of Christmas Eve, a signalman's error led to two trains colliding on the Settle and Carlisle line near Hawes Junction, the resultant fire kill-

ing 12 people. The bodies were taken to the nearby Moorcock Inn, the Board of Trade inquiry and the inquest convened at the same premises on Boxing Day – there presumably having been no room at the inn on Christmas Day. Times change.

The reporter at the Stanley inquest noted (and really shouldn't have done) that Nelly was a "pleasant, quiet-looking girl who listened with respect and composure throughout." The family, the report added, "had endeavoured to keep the affair as quiet as possible and so successfully that not even the next door neighbours were aware of the dreadful tragedy that had happened in the vicinity."

Nor, come to that, was PC Coates – the village bobby – and he lived just a few doors away.

The relevance of the fact that the deceased wasn't wearing trousers at the time of the assault is not immediately obvious, though the jury foreman appeared anxious to keep up with affairs. Was Billy Spencer drunk or sober, he asked the dead man's wife. "I think he'd had a drop" she replied, perhaps euphemistically.

The *Echo* was confident of a resolution. "Sergeant Smith, a shrewd and experienced officer is in charge of the case and may be trusted to make the fullest possible insight to it."

Concluding that it wasn't a case of murder, Mr Coroner Proud advised the jury to return a verdict of either manslaughter or accidental death, the panel opting for the former. Nelly, it was noted, showed "slight trepidation" but said nothing.

She was taken to Crook police station and the following day appeared before magistrates at Bishop Auckland. Her family unable to raise the "substantial" bail offered, the poor lass was taken off to Durham Gaol, there to await the Assizes.

What happened next is unknown but, day and night, Karl Utley is trying his hardest to find out.

Karl and Andrea had known one another since they were children but lost contact when he moved to Toft Hill – the place, remember, where the Lord Lieutenancy would have Baroness Armstrong ennobled - eight miles away on the A68. They met again at 28 – "she stalked me," says Karl – and were married six years later. They live in Crook, two miles below Stanley, his Mercedes convertible out the back.

Though she still keeps horses near the former Stanley Garden Centre it's Andrea who's disinclined to return to her roots and not even wild horses, says her husband, could drag her there. "It's isolated now, inconvenient for the children, they aren't independent yet," says Andrea. "It's all right for Karl, he knows everyone there."

He did, anyway. "I could walk down the back of Mount Pleasant and know everybody in every house except for about five. I still love walking around Stanley, it's just so serene and the paths around the old railway lines are so appealing. I love it. I'd buy or build a house at Jobson (Meadows) tomorrow if she'd come with me."

They also disagree over the extent to which community spirit has survived, though it's Andrea who believes that it's extant and her husband who supposes it extinct. The problem, he believes, is that so many of the older houses are now rented by folk unlikely to remain for long. "The majority of the older people have either died or gone on a pilgrimage to the Holy City" – by which Jerusalem, of course, he means Crook.

Might they themselves one day make the return journey? "One day I'd love to," says Karl, wistful of hearth and homecoming.

"Believe me," says Andrea – no less affectionately– "we're not."

The group's social media account – not so much a page, more a multi-faceted Facebook pictorial encyclopaedia – is a magic porridge pot, a bottomless treasure chest of nostalgic and infinite delights.

Amid the period pix are little jokey memories: when did you last eat crisp sandwiches, or get four for a penny, or see a policeman walking down the street? Remembering the Stanley winters, there's even a weather warning: "Southerners are urged not to travel unless absolutely necessary. Northerners, you'll need your big coat."

Inevitably there are ample Arctic images, too – snow up to the oxters, and sometimes up to the eaves – memories of bone broth and dumplings with which to counter the worst of it, improbable assertions from folk who still wish for wild winters like that.

There are plenteous pitmen, striking skies, magnificent vistas. There are teddy boys and steady boys, wakes, weddings and every fancy ball, with or without McNamara's Band. There's a picture of St Thomas's church with 22 men and boys in the choir and with an unsmiling vicar, a cutting about a Wooley miner who "missed a shift" and was thus on hand to save his family from a fire, a piece from *The Sun* about Britain's biggest Chuckle Brothers fan (about whom we shall be learning much more ere long.)

There's also a *Weardale Gazette* obituary on Kenny Ayre, born on the Hill Top in 1934 and all his life there – renowned artist, wood carver, spuggies a speciality – and author of the *Gazette's* much enjoyed "Clarty Walks" column. Kenny's mentioned in an earlier chapter, the chap who'd take an hour to get from one end of the front street to the other, such the volume of doorstep conversation.

From this wondrous cornucopia, however, perhaps the most intriguing image is of a banner-bearing parade formed up on the Heights of Alma, prompting one correspondent to suppose that, best suited, they might all have been marching off to Tow Law for the 1939 royal visit. Did the King and Queen really visit Tow Law? In its year-by-year chronicle, the Durham Rural Community Council confirms that indeed they did (that and a World War breaking out.)

It seems unlikely that so many would hoof that way, even if they'd missed the No 1 bus. If not quite an Orange march, could it have been a Masonic occasion – Stanley may never have had a lodge but Tow Law certainly has, and a Royal Arch, no less, chapter 3349, said to have been active for nearly 90 years.

As recently as June 2017 – clearly they'd heard about the winter weather - the internet records a visit to Tow Law Masonic Hall by the Third Provincial Grand Principal, the Provincial Deputy Grand Director of Ceremonies and goodness knows who else to honour Tom Simmons, "exalted" to the Royal Arch precisely fifty years earlier.

The likelihood, however, is that it was a Remembrance Day parade to the cenotaph, erected on the Heights of Alma in 1924. We'll salute that one in November.

It's six years since Karl posted on the Facebook page a glori-ously nostalgic, almost ecstatically emotional cine film of the dear old village around 1963 – just google "Stanley Crook" + Youtube. Even the music's a tear-jerker.

There's footage of the Billy Row Club trip to Redcar, red United buses nose to tail, men scrattin' about on the beach for sea coal – as if they hadn't enough at home– though possibly they fancied a crab. Since it was Redcar, it had been raining. Footage, too, of the working Stanley Incline, sports day at the Little House and of the 1963 Durham Miners' Gala, thronged by hundreds of thousands and addressed by Harold Wilson.

"We have become the natural party of government in this country" he tells the faithful on the Racecourse. They may have heard it before (and since.)

There are back street fights between kids armed with dustbin lids, weddings and wayzgooses, pigs not so much in clarts as in six feet of snow (and not looking very happy about it, either.) Snow's everywhere, as those who remember the winter of 1963 might well attest. The women folk shovel in their pinnies, the men – soft ha'porths – in top coats.

The highlight, however, yet more joyous than the club trip to Redcar, is the film of the Wooley pit ponies being brought up – lowsed out, as they may have said back then – for their own annual fortnight's holiday, the equine equivalent of Blackpool.

Put out to grass? For scenes of sheer joy – unbridled joy, it might appropriately be said – there has simply been nothing to compare. Do watch.

19: back to school

October 13 2021

Last night of all the good nights, the battery on the bedside alarm clock decided to die in my sleep. Due in class at 8 30am, for the first time in nearly sixty years I'm almost late for school.

Stanley Crook Primary School has been saluted in the first chapter: officially "outstanding" in many ways, seemingly just short of the pinnacle in others, "good" overall.

In 1990, when Durham County Council wanted to close it, the school had around 30 pupils. In 2011, when David Christie joined the staff for his first teaching job, there were twice as many. Two years later he became deputy head; in 2015, after just four years in teaching, he was appointed head teacher.

Now there are twice as many again, a pupil roll of 135, a capacity of 137 and a necessary catchment area of just 0.4 miles from the village. Once siblings are accommodated, there are about seven vacancies each year. It's an astonishing turnaround and, some might suggest, an astonishing reflection on the accustomed lack of vision of Durham County Council, a body which sometimes seems to possess all the foresight of the tail-end Charlie of the Gadarene swine.

Outstanding school children – the class of '21, pics by John Maughan

At much the same time as it proposed to pull out completely, the council sold the school house for £30,000. Now it's back on the market for £425,000. "We'd kill for the space" says the head.

Even before the first of several coffees in his office, however, I fall into conversation outside with Shaun Hope, school caretaker and owner of Britain's biggest collection of Chuckle Brothers memorabilia – "£30,000 worth, perhaps the biggest in the world," says Shaun. None might suppose otherwise.

He also has a pretty gruesome story about his grandmother, or some such forebear, who cut off her old feller's head. "My mother in Stanley still has the cuttings" he says. Breathlessly, bloodthirstily, it must all wait, though not for very long, upon another chapter.

I'm at school for the day, free to roam and to question, on the head's repeated recommendation particularly looking forward to school cook Carolyn Liddle's lunch. "Mrs Liddle's a local legend" says David. Her ginger biscuits are quite something, too.

It's too late, however, for the breakfast club, supervised by "breakfast buddies" and sponsored by Gregg's, the Newcastle-based bakery chain. For £1 a head it offers things like low sugar jam. whole wheat cereals, whole grain toast and semi-skimmed milk. No sign of steak bakes. In any case, it's so early in the day that I blearily wrote down "semi-skilled milk" and spend the next ten minutes wondering what a semi-skilled cow might achieve.

A rack of leaflets in the reception area embraces everything from *The Prevent strategy* – "a government strategy designed to stop people becoming terrorists or supporting terrorist and extreme causes" – to a little tract called *The Facts of Lice*. Innocent and intrigued, I may not be the first to misread the title.

At Timothy Hackworth Juniors in Shildon, the facts of life (if not of lice) were that you get the stick pretty much every day, that 50 crowded into a classroom suitable for about half as many and that the female of the species seemed pretty much an irrelevance (save, perhaps, for postman's knock.)

What swiftly becomes apparent in this 148-year-old school building, now physically detached from the village itself, is how totally education provision has changed. What becomes irresistible is comparison with those long-lost days at Tin

Kitchen queen – Carolyn Liddle

Tacks, as universally the Shildon school was known. This place doesn't even smell of school, or at least not of boiled cabbage, with which in the 1950s the school day was pretty much synonymous.

There are no rows of desks, no raised voices, no chalk, much talk. While there may be any amount of wise young owls, there are no parrots. "We don't have 135 robots, we have 135 individual characters" says the head. While there is carrot, and not just in Mrs Liddle's luscious lunches, there is emphatically no stick – neither here nor anywhere else, of course.

Mr Christie produces a "Punishment book", starting in the 1920s, in which – shamelessly, sedulously and ultimately unsuccessfully – I search for the name of Ernest Armstrong, a future leader of church and state and perhaps a pre-war goody two shoes.

For climbing on a flat roof to retrieve a ball, an unfortunate boy received two strokes on the hand – and for "encouraging" him, his mate the same. For interfering with a teacher's tin of pins at playtime, clearly a more reprehensible offence, a wretched child received two on each hand, as did the boy who stole goosegogs from the school garden and his mate who ran around the shrubbery.

Breaking a branch from an apple tree – patently Stanley's youngsters knew little of environmental friendships – brought two on the hand and more on the "seat", though the boy who opened the door to the budgie's cage received but one of the best.

Whether the budgie was in residence at the time, whether punishment would have been more severe had it been, is sadly not recorded.

David also digs out elderly "sales" books showing that the school received a mere £1 for "condemned furniture" but that it appeared to have a lucrative side-line in peg bags. Admission registers, similarly historic, record not just the date of a child's arrival but the reason for departure. Some have gone down hill to Peases West, some a little more widely into the world. A worrying number over the years had left for the fairly inescapable reason that they had died, scarlet fever often deemed responsible.

Altogether greater emphasis on health and wellbeing now exists among 5-11-year-olds, not least mental health, enshrined in the mantra that it's all right not to be all right. Why else would the school employ a Worry Wizard, a qualified child psychologist, every Friday afternoon?

"At Stanley Crook" says the school website "we absolutely love a mindfulness Zenden. It helps us relax and feel calm." It's what they call a "calming strategy" and is something to which we shall return.

It's also at once evident that David remembers every one of his 135 charges by their first names, seamlessly shifting to "Sunshine" – or, on one occasion to "Sweetheart" – if momentarily he lapses. He remembers most of the parents' names, too. "The staff are all the same" he says, a feat made yet more impressive by the fertile array of forenames on offer. At Tin Tacks we were chiefly Michael or David (unless, of course, of the opposite sex). Here they range from Aaron to Zak and others like Jensen, Preston, Torin, Mila, Coleson and Cormack. "Remembering them comes naturally" he insists.

Frequently he high-fives the bairns, sometimes simply applauds them. It never happened at post-war Tin Tacks, unless high fives was a knuckle sandwich. A little lad in the second group whispers in the 21st century vernacular. "Our school" he says "is mint."

Among the documents from the back of the cupboard, there's also a thick sheaf of parents' protest letters – "dismayed" to

Head way – David Christie

"disgusted" and much damnation between times – at the closure proposal in 1990. Around the community there's now a general acceptance that if the village school had gone, Stanley Hill Top would slowly but certainly have disappeared with it. That's quite a statement.

David Christie, now 41, was born and raised in South Shields, played cricket for Durham County junior sides from 13 to 17, looked set for a successful financial services career before an unexpected change of direction. "I'd often thought of becoming a teacher when I was younger" he says.

He did a belated A-level in psychology – "me among all those 16-and-17-year-olds" – gained a first class education degree at Durham University and after four years out for family reasons interviewed for his first teaching post at Stanley.

What did he know of the place? "Very little, though I'd seen signs to it on the way to playing cricket at Crook. I knew there were some deprivation issues but really not much more than that. I was just glad to get a job – they took a long shot with me."

Thereafter his progress was bullet-fast – deputy head after two years, though still a classroom teacher, appointed to succeed head teacher Shirley Oswald at the end of 2015. "Shirley's parting words to me were always to look out for the children," he says. "I've never forgotten them."

He lives near Durham, is married with a 17-year-old daughter, Holly. "I try to run the school as if Holly were here" he says. "I have the same ambitions for every one of the children here as I have for Holly."

For half of the week he's also now acting head at Woodhouse

Close primary school in Bishop Auckland and very likely headed for other, higher, things. "The jungle drums have started beating" he admits, "but I'd be very sad to leave here."

Much of the ethos – one of the head's favourite words, another is "challenging" – is embraced by the impressive website, cogently and concisely communicated. "The curriculum" it says "is dynamic, creative, meaningful and FUN." Save for an acronym avalanche, "fun" is the only word in capitals. "The head teacher" the website adds, "takes a keen interest in curriculum development and refining pedagogical application." Probably they talk of little else in Billy Row Club.

If not from A-to-Z – nothing about Zenden mindfulness – dozens of "policies" range from asthma to whistle blowing, though not penny whistle blowing. There's a grammar, spelling and punctuation policy, too, its success evident in the mission statement, though the "spirituality" policy says nothing about Christianity. "You have to be careful with some parents" says David. "We don't want to be seen to promote one religion over another. We seek to promote tolerance and understanding."

Though harvest festival at St Thomas's is upcoming, they also make visits to a synagogue in Gosforth, have links with the Islam Society in Durham and learn about other faiths.

The five year groups are divided into "Teams" – a happy acronym for Together Everyone Achieves More – each named after children's authors like Morpurgo, Cowell, Dahl, Walliams and Donaldson. There was a Team Rowling, too, until – as David puts it – "she made a couple of comments." Best say no more.

The head is charismatic, communicative, clearly collegiate and highly enthusiastic – "a dream" says Carolyn Liddle, 28 years

at the school, with whom a mutual appreciation society has evidently been formed (and whose pork steaks suggest that Mr Christie was right about that, an' all.)

Carolyn, now widowed, moved up from Willington 30 years ago, still has two adult daughters on the Hill Top. "We love it, I think it's the people and the community spirit" she says. "There isn't much else, is there?"

The Ofsted inspection, the first under Mr Christie's leadership, had been in 2019. That the school narrowly failed to win an overall "outstanding" rating clearly, perhaps euphemistically, disappoints him. "My biggest regret was for the staff, those guys really deserved it. It was a good school but I think we improved it, made it fit for the 21st century and got some fantastic results.

"To say that I was gutted for the staff would probably be an understatement. If she (the inspector) hadn't graded personal development and pupil behaviour outstanding, I'd have been fuming. We were very pleased she recognised that."

His annual budget, carefully controlled, is £811,000 – of which just £5,000 is allocated to capital maintenance. "For a 148-year-old building it's not bad at all" he says, and credits Shaun Hope for keeping the place in good nick. He'd also been quoted £4,000 for a new electronic bell system. "£4,000 for a bell? I'd rather spend it on the children."

The school also had to spend £2,000 on road signs outside after pupils successfully joined the battle to halve the speed limit from 60mph.

Sport embraces everything from golf to tag rugby. The website paragraph on spiritual development mentions nothing about

God (or gods) but talks of "the growth of pupils' sense of self, their unique potential, their understanding of their strengths and weaknesses and their will to achieve."

The head accepts the argument that, save for the school, the village itself might no longer be standing. "A chap who was moving into a new house told me they'd only come to Stanley because of the school, which was very kind of him. It does seem possible that if it weren't for the school, there might hardly be a village at all."

A tour underlines that Ofsted was spot on about behaviour.

The bairns are brilliant, engaged seemingly without exception, polite to a point, confident not cowed. The week previously they'd had Richard Holden, the area's newish Conservative MP, in. "I think he was impressed" says David.

The walls are covered – every available inch, or so it seems – with pupils' artwork, spooky reminders that Hallowe'en is just a fortnight away and images of war, "We do a lot of work with the Royal British Legion" says David. "Every child in the school knows something about the First World War."

Community initiatives include litter picking, though not in the

Old school - 1922

woods across the fields at the back. "Too many needles" says David. "We tell the council about those."

The head seems particularly keen on the outdoor area at the front – the forest school – with play equipment, plants, a construction area, workout gear, a fire pit and what he supposes the biggest sandpit known to man. There's a bug hotel, too – "the children just put their hands in and see what they come up with" he says. "I run a mile. Mrs Martin finishes her outdoor class with toasted marshmallows; wonderful."

Almost everyone, he says, has computer technology at home. "It's vital but in a way we're reversing that. We want to make them familiar with the environment and they love getting outside." It doesn't help that the school's broadband speeds are "terrible."

There are groups like Discovery Club, Super Movers, Cosmic Kids, Mood Walks, yoga and Go-noodles. Whatever Go-noodles is, their speciality appears to be something called "banana banana meatballs."

Back inside, Vicki Williams's science class is making a circuit, or circuits (which, apparently, have nothing to do with Scalextric.) I tell her that after 55 years in journalism, this is the first interview and assignment in which I've needed a second notebook. "I'm surprised Mr Christie kept it to two" she says.

While still headmaster, he'd once had to cover Mrs Williams's class for two terms. "It nearly killed me" he claims.

So what do the children like about it all? "My three favourite things are reading English, maths and sport" says Jacob, who may have to work a bit harder on the maths. "If you're down the teachers pick you up" says Oliver, "sharing" says Geor-gia, "fish and chips on Fridays" says Hannah, "how supportive teachers are" says Luke, "being yourself" says Janet. "Everything" says Ben, in summary.

Asked what might most enhance their village, opinion is divided between a Primark and a McDonald's, neither of which seems particularly imminent (though there's an ice cream van some days.)

Mr Christie, still present, is also the designated "safeguarding lead". Again he reminds them that if there are any problems they should talk to a staff member. "I love to come to work, I really do, you're a social worker, a GP, a psychologist, a policeman and a business manager but the kids are absolutely fantastic and we always have their backs. I want everyone else to love being here, too, because when I left school in South Shields I never wanted to go near the place again."

"If we can teach them that it's all right not to be all right, all right to get things wrong, obviously in an age-appropriate way, it will make them strong and resilient. There's no point in coming to school and being miserable. We're light years ahead of other schools in developing that approach.

"The former expectations of children at stages seven and eight are now what we expect at stages one and two, The biggest problem is trying to fit everything in. I think our core ethos and values strike a real chord with parents."

A final coffee and I head for home shortly before the bairns. Probably like them, I've learned a great deal today.

20: band aid

October 15 2021

The evening temperature's not so much hovering above freezing as shivering above it. It's just one degree Centigrade and no matter that Co Durham folk suppose it backend-ish, it's still only mid-October, for heaven's sake. Smoke from a residual fire in the Aged Miners' Homes rises clear and vertical, some houses already fairy-lit, though whether for a hobnob Hallowe'en or a frighteningly early Christmas is uncertain. The views, of course, are quite wonderful.

At the parish church, by contrast, things – however figuratively – are warming up nicely: an attempt to raise short-term funds to keep St Thomas's open a little longer, the Bearpark and Esh Colliery Band is playing – without charge – its first indoor concert since the original lockdown.

"It's absolutely jumping in there" someone says as I head, half-perished, up the path.

"Chocker" confirms another.

None uses the term "wick", the word in that sense now almost obsolete, though Stanley may seldom have seen so big or so enthusiastic a crowd since the road past the Aged Miners was wick with folk in the hour before a United derby match with Crook.

They've baked, and it looks good, but perhaps not in anticipation of feeding the five thousand.

Many are mufflered, like Bob Cratchit crouched around the last faint spark of his master's parsimony. Soon they will be further warmed, perhaps even strangely warmed (as John Wesley supposed of the hour of his Aldersgate enlightenment.)

The band, augmented by musicians from elsewhere, gives it real what fettle (another phrase which may seldom be heard in 2021). They're magnificent, the programme ranging from *Dear Lord and Father of Mankind* to *Chitty Chitty Bang-Bang* and from *Lord of all hopefulness* – favourite hymn of the lady of this house – to the Elvis Presley song *Can't help falling in love*, more recently appropriated by followers of Sunderland Football Club.

Pam Oliver says how lovely is it to see the church filled and so, of course, it is. Acoustically it's brilliant, too – "a fantastic place to play" says Phil Tait, the band's musical director – again prompting the thought of how greatly the community might miss this place and what, with a bit of fresh thinking, might be done to redeem and to rehabilitate it.

Janet Charlton and her long time friend Evelyn Johnson are camped around a pretty ineffectual heater at the back. Now 69, Janet was just 18 months old when her parents moved down from Cornsay Colliery after buying the village general dealer's – or one of them, at any rate. Frank Hogan ran a travelling shop, too, and for many years was an official of Stanley United and principal benefactor of the Stanley Development Fund.

"Every week he'd provide the raffle prizes" Janet recalls. "A 3lb ham, 3lb pork, 3lb beef, cost him a fortune, daft bugger."

Janet herself worked for 40 years in the special care baby unit at Bishop Auckland General Hospital – "some of them babbies still come to see me" – but on Saturdays found herself running the life saving United tea hut, its function similar to that of a thermal blanket and purveyor of the finest cup of Bovril since the Pope was deemed infallible. Barry Johnson, Evelyn's late husband, did all manner of jobs around the ground, too, Evelyn never far away to help.

Janet lived a couple of doors down from Dave and Doris Ayre, subject of an earlier chapter, before they settled in the care home at Billy Row. "I really miss them" she says. "I'd always be baking for them, taking stuff around. It's not the same, baking for one."

She also tells the story of the long-gone day when a well dressed stranger – "cavalry twill coat, the lot" – walked into the Hill Top shop, supposedly seeking directions to Darlington. "Me dad thought he was a burglar, casing the place, was all for calling the polliss until me mam told him not to be so daft. Next night we saw the same feller on telly, Marty Wilde the singer. Can you believe, Marty Wilde in our shop. I still bet me dad sold him summat, though."

She greatly worries about the church closure. "It would be terrible, awful. This village these days has nowt, nowt except a post box. People just won't come to things." The pair of them, says Evelyn without argument, are as guilty as anyone. Mind, she adds, it could do with being a bit warmer.

Like the dumplings at old school dinners, though not of course Mrs Liddle's, the best is saved till last. Phil Tait having donned a rather natty Union Jack waistcoat for the purpose, the band plays the finale from Last Night of the Proms – *Fantasia of British Sea Songs, Land of Hope and Glory, Jerusalem* and that jaunty number which sounds like it should be *Thine be the glory*, Christendom's finest hymn, but probably isn't. They even give out little plastic flags, perhaps a job lot from the pound shop down in Crook. The gathering positively whoops. Waving

not drowning? It's greatly to be hoped.

Some of the splendid bairns, encountered so prim and properly at the village school just two days earlier, are literally, joyfully, dancing in the aisles. Stanley may not have had a better night since the day the Queen was crowned.

At the end, the Rev Geoff Lawes tells them that the fight is still on – as if anyone doubted St Thomas's – and that they won't be giving up. "It's my favourite church of all those I've worked in" says the retired priest, as he had that sunny Sunday morning in mid-August, adding that so long as the doors remained open, they'd all be very welcome.

The band will be back, together with the Crook and Weardale Choral Society, for a Christmas special on December 21. Unless there's six feet of snow, unless hell or the Hill Top freezes over – the latter perhaps more likely – then so, most certainly, shall I.

21: Chuckle vision

October 21 2021

Barely a week since bumping into Shaun Hope outside the village school where he's the highly regarded caretaker, I'm sitting as cold evening falls in his mum's front room on the Hill Top, discussing everything from the Chuckle Brothers to murder most foul and wondering where on earth to start.

Christine Winter – Joan Hope's sister, Shaun's aunt – is also there. "I think the Chuckle Brothers are stupid" she says.

"I've laughed at them but not very often" says Joan.

"It's just something different, isn't it?" says Shaun, by no means deferentially but aware that his hobby may to others seem a little – what shall we say? – improbable. "I know it might sound a bit daft but I don't smoke and I don't drink, this is my hobby. I'm thinking about starting a Krankies collection next."

There's also uncomfortable reminiscence about Joan's child-

Laugh a minute – Shaun Hope and friends

hood – "locked away for eight years in a sanatorium" – and of the good old bad old days among the oft-bleak pit terraces . Firstly, though, let's revisit the dark days of October 1936 and no laughing matter at all.

Sarah Ann Simpson, a 21-year-old Stanley lass, had married Thomas Manuel, an unemployed miner seven years her senior, in the summer of 1935. It proved not to be a happy relationship, though nothing could have foreshadowed its terrible ending.

Some things might seem almost familiar – the poverty, the jealousy, the booze. What might surprise a 21st century reader, however, is the speed at which officialdom's wheels whirred thereafter.

Poor Sarah, who'd miscarried some months previously, was brutally beaten to death with a hammer in the early hours of Saturday October 10, though her body wasn't discovered until shortly after 2pm the following Monday. Her husband lay dead in the next room, killed by a self-administered overdose of disinfectant. A blood trail was spattered between them, a note to his mother lay by the killer's side.

"Dear Mother. Forgive me as I loved her but she did not love me. She told me the bairn was not mine, so we will both go together. Give my love to the two bairns and ask father to be good to you. Your loving son Tom." The note was followed by a line of crosses.

"When the note was read" said *The Northern Echo's* inquest report, "the dead man's mother showed great distress and had to be led from the room."

The inquest had been opened and concluded the day after the bodies were found, the funerals held two days after that –

Bed fellows – part of Shaun's shrine

Sarah taken from the family home in Wooley Terrace through a bible-black throng of mourners to St Thomas's church and interred in the graveyard. Thomas was buried in Crook.

A similar example of how the pace of change sometimes goes backwards had come in 1902 following the death in a pony and trap accident of father-of-seven Martin Button, described as "butcher and farmer" and living between Stanley and Waterhouses. The inquest was held at the Wooley Inn – the White City – the day after his death, the funeral at Brancepeth parish church again just two days after that. Forty-seven vehicles and a great multitude on foot followed the hearse.

Today the funerals would have taken the best part of a month to authorise and the inquest a year. It gave new meaning to the Prayer Book phrase about the quick and the dead.

The bodies of Sarah and Tom Manuel were found in an end-of-terrace pit cottage in California Terrace, Bowden Close – a colliery community between Crook and Wooley – into which the couple had moved just a few weeks earlier. They'd spent the Friday evening with family in Stanley, leaving after midnight – perhaps after a good drink – on the 30-minute walk home.

Some time afterwards a neighbour had heard screaming but took it to be a dog growling – or so he told the inquest – turned over and went back to sleep. Tom Manuel was seen about the area on both the Saturday and Sunday, on one occasion trying to sell a neighbour a goat – perhaps for money to buy the fatal disinfectant, it was surmised. Scratches on his face, he explained, had been caused by falling into a bush.

Sarah had apparently wanted to join an outing to Blackpool, in those days the first resort. Tom, said at the social services centre he attended to be a quiet man, wouldn't allow it. Possessiveness may have been at the heart of it. "Even if the poor lass went out the back for some coal he'd want to know who she'd been talking to" says Joan Hope. Though the couple had twice separated, on one occasion for five months, they were said to be trying again.

Fond farewell – Sarah Manuel's cortege at Wooley Terrace

The coroner, Mr J E Brown-Humes – a family name still greatly remembered in south Durham legal circles – offered the jury observations on the nature of the green-eyed god. "You know that jealousy is one of the strongest passions and most unreasonable of human mentality. It finally ate into this man's very soul. From the very early stages of their marriage, this unfortunate man was possessed of a most unreasonable jealousy and I think you will be satisfied that there are no reasons for believing that Mrs Manuel was unfaithful to her husband."

Whether the inquest was in a miner's cottage in Bowden Close or some impersonal office in Bishop Auckland is, sadly, not recorded. Verdicts of murder and of suicide duly were.

After so gruesome an interlude, the Chuckle Brothers may seem like laugh-a-minute – which to Shaun Hope they undoubtedly were – the past tense necessary because Barry Elliott, the elder of the siblings, died in 2018. Paul survives him.

Shaun had first seen them at the Darlington Civic Theatre pantomime in 2001, there with his son and a party from Stanley school. The pantomime was Goldilocks, audience members required temporarily to take the part of the three bears. It proved something of a honey trap, the first time – first of thirty or four, Shaun reckons – that one or other of the Chuckle Brothers had deposited a custard pie in his face. "Afterwards" he says "I got given a few bits and pieces and I was hooked."

Shaun and family have recently moved from Willington to Crook; the incredible collection is in temporary storage at his mum's. "If there's ever a fire it won't be the furniture I'll have to save first, it'll be that lot in the spare bedroom" says Joan, who's 78.

A Twitter line somewhere supposed it one of the biggest Chuckle Brothers collections in the world, offering the perhaps optimistic presumption that there were others.

It really is quite astonishing, for all that – posters to programmes, mouse mats to fridge magnets, clothes to credit cards, teddy bears to trousers – underpants, too – jelly babies to jigsaw puzzles. All are Chuckle Brothers themed, most are signed by one or both of the brethren. There's even one of Barry's leather jackets – "the one he did Cher in" says Shaun. What definitely aren't autographed are 7,000 Civic Theatre flyers from another Chuckle extravaganza. "They were just going to throw them out and asked if I wanted them" says Shaun. "If I sold them on eBay for £2 each I

Mr and Mrs Manuel.

Tragic couple –
Thomas and Sarah Manuel

could make £14,000."

Might there be another 7,000 Chuckle Brotherly lovers out there? "I'm sure there are quite a few" he says.

His passion has brought several television appearances of his own, numerous newspaper articles and even became a question on the BBC Television show *Have I Got News For You*, still stored on his smartphone. "Ken Livingstone got it right" he recalls.

He not only helped organise a petition to bring back Chucklevision, which ran to 294 shows – "though I preferred the stage shows" – but another to have the pair present *The Great British Bake-off*. Back in 2011 he'd told the *Echo* that his sons – Ben,

then 15, and Jak who was nine – were also keen followers. Still hooked? "They've grown up a bit" says Shaun.

The entertainers, born in Rotherham, passionate Rotherham United supporters, had been unfailingly helpful. "Nothing's ever been a problem to them. I've been backstage many times and in their dressing rooms many times. I even got invited to Barry's funeral. It's really just a joke about the Krankies. Whatever happens, I'll always be a Chuckle Brothers man now."

Born on the Hill Top, diagnosed with spinal TB when just five, Joan Hope spent the next eight years in a sanatorium at Earls House, near Durham, sent work from the village school at Stanley. She didn't attend until 13. "I spent all that time in a plaster cast, a lot of it on a board," she recalls. "I'm sure I was drugged; it explains why I now spend half my time lying on the floor."

The little table is piled high with sweets for when the bairns come trick-or-treating, many windows in the long village terraces frit with Hallowe'en horribilia, though it doesn't need pound shop ghosts and ghoulies to feel the October evening chill on the Hill Top.

Finally back home, Joan was one of five children living in her grandparents' two-up two-down, and none of the rooms what might be supposed spacious. "We had no hot water, no flushing toilet just a wooden thing out the back, coal house across the back street. It was terrible in winter. Everything had to be boiled and everyone used the same water, except when my granddad came home from the pit about four o'clock in the morning. Everything had still to be ready for him, though; he'd be filthy.

INQUEST VERDICT

MAN'S FAREWELL NOTE TO HIS MOTHER

THE tiny mining hamlet known as Bowden Close, between Crook and Wooley, was on Monday the scene of a shocking tragedy.

Shortly after 2 p.m. the dead bodies of a young married couple were found in their locked-up house in California Terrace. They were : Thomas Manuel, aged 30, an unemployed miner, and his wife, Sarah Ann Manuel, aged 23. The woman was found in bed with terrible injuries to her head. A hammer with which the wounds had apparently been inflicted was found near the bed, which was saturated with blood.

In the kitchen Manuel was found stretched on a mat. He had died from disinfectant poisoning. A bottle containing disinfectant was found on the table. There was every indication that a struggle had taken place, for there was a trail of blood leading from the kitchen to the sitting-room, where the body of Mrs Manuel was found.

Inquest verdict

"I was 21 before I got my first new coat. If anyone had anything they didn't want, they'd just say 'Give it to Joan'."

Christine remembers those days, too. "Sometimes we had a bath on a Friday, whether we needed one or not, sometimes we didn't. If you were last in, you were just washing in clarts. Honest, we must have stunk."

Joan's difficult childhood has residual effect. "I'm still frightened of everyone – frightened of doctors, frightened of policemen, frightened of teachers. I haven't been on a bus for forty years because of it."

So how had she spent her leisure time? "I had five bairns in six years, Shaun was the youngest. You didn't have leisure time, I don't think I even got on the club trip. Mind, I did once or twice get down to Crook."

Christine remembers bleak mid-winters, remembers Mr Hall, the school headmaster, who lived in Sunniside, a mile or so west. "If it was really bad he'd come into school on skis, the snow wouldn't stop him The miners would dig a path for us to get there, too. We never missed a day because of the weather. It was a nice school but very strict. Even if you were playing outside in the street and a teacher came by, you'd stand up to attention until they'd passed."

Were they really the good old days? The sisters' answer is almost synchronised, could almost have come from the Chuckle Brothers: "You have to be bloody well joking."

22: royal family

October 26 2021

A strange little procession meanders its way around Newton Aycliffe, the once-new town north of Darlington. Comfortably wrapped in a wheelchair at its head is 90-year-old Freda Tinkler, formerly Pinkney, one of old Stanley's best remembered families.

Who might have known that the 1911 census listed four Isaac Pinkneys on the Hill Top, and probably every one of them answering more familiarly to Ike?

Behind Freda, pushing valiantly, is her niece Anita Atkinson MBE, former local newspaper editor and owner of the world's richest panoply of Royal Family memorabilia, a collection which in its majesty and magnificence makes Shaun Hope's otherwise remarkable Chuckle Brotherhood resemble by comparison a few odds and ends in a shoebox. More of those crown jewels shortly.

Next in line come Anita's friend Lilian and, perpetually at the rear, an elderly author – on-the-hoof shorthand yet more incomprehensible than usual, questions more erratic, ears straining to catch the answers above the Tuesday morning traffic. Periodically as he writes he walks into a bush and bears the scratches to suggest as much; on one occasion he has a near-death experience with a concrete lamp post. It never happened to J K Rowling.

Freda lives in a nearby care home, where visitors are for good reason still not encouraged. As the curious cavalcade continues, she thinks she detects a bit of sleet in the breeze and, of course, has long experience of such unseasonal assaults. Her memory's vivid: it's a most enjoyable morning.

Freda was second youngest of nine children of Isaac and Annie Pinkney, of whom only she survives. Her father was a miner who also worked Wooley Bridge Farm, found time to support and sometimes to play for Stanley United but little for what might these days be termed social graces.

"I was always glad when he went to watch the football, it got him out of the house for a bit" Freda recalls at about 3mph. "My mother couldn't do anything with him, he always got his own way. A lot of people had no time for my dad because he had a temper and fought with folk. He was a hard worker, but expected everyone else to work hard, too."

Particularly she remembers the morning when her father told her to get in the car, an early Standard 8, "I thought we were going for a ride out somewhere but we ended up at the court, where he'd been charged with watering the milk and he told them it was me who did it. He had no scruples: if he could blame someone else and get off himself, he would."

On another occasion the young Freda was returning from a friend's when she saw a crowd gathered outside their house – "just part of a terrace" – and realised that it was on fire. Responsibility was laid on one of her siblings, playing in a cupboard with matches. "I remember a little black doll sitting on the bedroom window ledge, melting, and my sister crying" she says.

Temporarily homeless, some of the family were accommodated at the Miners Arms in Billy Row – the affectionately remembered Nicky's – run for many years by Billy Nicholson, her Uncle William, though he himself was strictly teetotal. Alice, his wife, wouldn't so much as set foot in the licensed part of the house.

"I think they must have been Methodists" says Freda, "but I liked Uncle William. He was different."

"He'd serve beer to most of Billy Row and Stanley while quietly drinking his half of lemonade" remembers Anita.

Though other family members were offered emergency accommodation, however, Ikey Pinkney was in every sense barred out. "No one wanted us next door to them, either" says Freda. "That was my dad, too. He was a queer bugger, my dad. Mind, I think the Nicholsons maybe thought of us as secondary citizens, sort of, because we were miners. They probably thought my mother had married beneath her. We were always a bit like gypsies, you know."

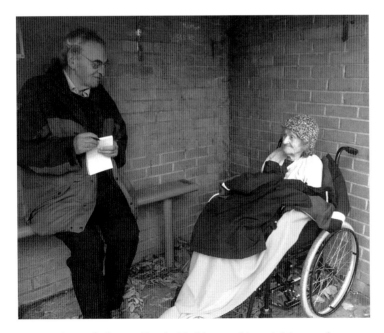

Taking shelter – Freda Tinkler and inquisitive author

Eventually the family was put up at Wooley Bridge Farm, a nine-acre holding where Ike kept cows, hens, a few horses and at least one goat. "He cooked the goat at a particularly bad time when they'd no money to buy anything else" says Anita. "None of the kids would eat it because it was their pet."

Family folklore also has it that, similarly claiming hardship, Ike had once gone to Ernest Armstrong's councillor father – also known as Sikey, which explains an old puzzle – seeking help. Armstrong told him to go the poor house. "Ike flattened him" says Freda. There may also have been a Tinkler's cuss.

She herself had been baptised at St Thomas's, educated between the ages of five and 14 at the village school – "I remember Mr Taylorson and Mr Rosethorn, nice teachers, but I didn't much care for some of the others" – met and married Cyril Tinkler, a Roman Catholic miner at Roddymoor Colliery who lived down the bank in Crook. Freda declined to convert to Catholicism and was told that the church wedding would only go ahead without music and bells and that they'd have to leave the church by the back door. They went to the register office instead. Cyril was later among the many who travelled to help the rescue effort after the Aberfan pit heap disaster in Wales.

Life on Stanley Terrace had remained arduous, overcrowded and insanitary, at one point compelling Anita's father Joe to run away from home – to pedal away, at any rate, knapsack on his back and brother Jim on the crossbar. They'd almost got as far as Willington – all of two miles away – before deciding like the ancients they that might fall off the end of the world and turning round again.

Anita's aunt Florrie and uncle Norman did get as far as America, however, though they came back on the *Queen Mary* after the UK National Health Service was founded. "It was cheaper for them to get a return ticket on the *Queen Mary* than it was for them to get all their medical supplies in America" Freda insists. "They went back with half a dozen pairs of glasses, dentures, all sorts."

Such was the Pinkneys' progress. Until recently, Anita believed her eldest granddaughter to be Ike's 100th direct descendant until discovering that she had an unknown brother, Arnold, in the Durham area.

Joe had himself been a miner – "he talked of walking across the field in tears for his first shift when he was 14, terrified of the pit but even more terrified of going home to tell his dad he hadn't gone" – and then a driver for the Tow Law-based Baldwin and Barlow bus company. While there, though probably not behind the wheel, he had an affair with a clippy (prompting the unworthy thought on the Newton Aycliffe perambulation that she may only have been a clippy but that she was clearly just the ticket.) Arnold, adopted, had tracked down his kin with the help of Durham library.

"He's lovely" says Anita, and no matter that her granddaughter has dropped from100th to 104th in the line of descendants. "All us Pinkneys keep in touch, even the one going around the world on a yacht" she adds. "We're probably all a bit eccentric."

So the crocodile continues, finally seeking refuge, as Anita's photograph illustrates, in a benevolent bus shelter. Freda had long been resident in Newton Aycliffe before moving into the care home and is probably glad to be back there, Her heart, if nothing else, remains warm.

"It's been lovely" she says and so, bless her, it has.

Such Anita Atkinson's passion for the royal family, such her red-white-and-blue blood, that to mark the Queen's silver jubilee in 2012 she opened Royal Teas in Stanhope – a summer-long café in which every inch was festooned with monarchical memorabilia. What happened next made headlines around the world.

Every afternoon at 3pm she'd invite a visiting youngster to tap a helium balloon which, thus encouraged, would play the National Anthem and all present would be invited to stand. Three middle-aged women not only declined to get to their feet but continued gossiping throughout – and Anita, little more than 5ft tall, wasn't standing for that, either. She threw them out. "If they'd been leather clad bikers or young yobs you'd have expected to call the police" she says.

The British royal family being pretty busy in 2012, the tea toom had been opened by Princess Helen of Romania (who, memory suggests, lived somewhere near Esh Winning.) Its theme left nothing to the imagination: even the toilets had thrones (though gags about the royal wee were probably frowned upon, too.)

The tea room – "It's not a business, it's an event" Anita had insisted – proved hugely, almost overwhelmingly, popular. "I've found myself turning into Basil Fawlty and insulting people left, right and centre because I was so stressed out" she said at the time.

Royal Teas, as always intended, closed at that end of the summer. The middle-aged republicans never returned.

Her parents had moved down to Billy Row – locals would suppose it Grahamsley – her frequent talks to local organisations entitled From Billy Row to Buckingham Palace.

Her regal obsession had begun in 1977 when, for her birthday, someone gave her a pack of Silver Jubilee playing cards. By the time of her marriage to John Atkinson two years later, life was turning into a royal command performance. Until the weather intervened, the bridesmaids were to have worn red, white and blue and the cake was in the shape of the Imperial State Crown.

It was March 17, the first day of British Summer Time, though such considerations seldom worried the west Durham weather gods. The bride – and the rest of the county – woke to something more like a scene from a Christmas card. "I looked out of the window for my little MG and all I could see was the top of the aerial" she says. "People always said it would be a snowy day before I got married."

The bridesmaids wore wellies, someone dropped the cake, just 30 of the 170 invited guests made it through the blizzard with many obliged to spend the night on the floor of the wedding venue, the Elite Hall in Crook. "They were sackless" says Anita, as County Durham folk do, and with little thought for etymology.

Happily, the police were able to clear a road so John and Anita could head off on honeymoon – perhaps inevitably at the Royal County Hotel.

Two years later the birth of Ruth, their first child, coincided with the wedding of Charles and Diana. Anita took flags and bunting into the maternity ward – a double celebration.

She has attended several royal garden parties, was appointed MBE for services to the monarchy, is acknowledged by *Guinness World Records* to have the biggest royal collection on the planet. In 2011 she camped for two nights outside Westminster Abbey in order better to get a view of William and Catherine's wedding but hasn't always offered unquestioning allegiance.

Dismayed by the departure of Harry and Meghan – "I really can't be bothered with either of them" – she was never too enamoured of the People's Princess, either. The Queen remains – well – majestic.

Anita's 65, grandmother of four, a deputy lieutenant of County Durham and a hard working magistrate. Whatever eccentricities she may suppose, she's a lovely, lively ever-helpful lady who recently converted an old dairy barn on their farm near Crook into a royal museum with more than 12,000 items dating from 1760. Most have been donated. The collection's said to be worth more than the farmhouse is and has proved greatly popular.

Royal tea - Anita Atkinson

"Britishness is on the school curriculum now" says Anita. "My personal aim is to promote the monarchy and educate people on the constitutional role it plays."

She's now writing a book about her eight years in the control room of Durham County Fire Brigade – " a lovely time" – and further expanding her collection. Her Majesty's platinum anniversary is at hand. It will be roundly toasted by Anita Atkinson, the subject of it all.

Pretty in Pinkney - sisters Nellie, Joy, Audrey, Anne, Freda and Elaine line up for their wedding photographer

23: lest we forget

November 14 2021:

Though the guns fell silent at the 11th hour of the 11th day of the 11th month, that great time of Remembrance in the villages around Stanley Hill Top can't always be synchronised – lots of war memorials, too few clergy simultaneously to officiate.

Remembrance – Stanley War Memorial

If not at the going down of the sun then most certainly in the morning, Stanley's commemoration is held at 9am, the weather yet to make its mind up. "It's not raining, it's not windy, it's beautiful" says Catherine Lawes, the officiating Church of England lay reader, inarguably adding that few war memorials could have a view like that one.

"Usually it's a gale force breeze" says someone else, recalling that Doris Ayre always wore a pin in her hat. "If she hadn't it would have been blowing all the way down the bank." Today's visibility, however, may best be described as limited.

A dozen or so people and a respectful dog are gathered around the granite memorial, erected at a cost of £435 and unveiled in 1924 by Sir Arthur Pease. Atop it is the figure of a woman, said to be dressed in "classic drapery" and holding a wreath. Different accounts describe her pose as "sorrowful" and "dejected".

One face lists the 43 local men – and Ethel Winship, a solitary woman – who died during World War I, almost half from the Durham Light Infantry. Another has the names of 19 who fell during World War II.

Save in the case of Ethel Winship, the surname is suffixed by initials and then the initials of their regiment. Ethel Winship's name is followed by the initials MW, a puzzle until the following day, when for the second time in the course of the Stanley story I'm pointed towards Vera Ryder – Ethel Winship's niece.

MW was munitions worker, not front line but greatly hazardous, nonetheless. Ethel, unmarried, had been killed at a factory in Newcastle. "I don't think she was very old at all" says Vera. "People forget, don't they?"

The Sunday morning turnout appears apathetic at best, a

further question mark over "community". The church folk, conversely, are encouraged. "Sometimes it's only two or three" says Pam Oliver.

One of them is Kevin Heslop, recently shifted from his lifelong haunts around Stanley to a bungalow in Crook. "The winters were getting ower card" he says which, converted into Celsius, means that it can get a bit fresh up there. "Nee more climbing stairs, nee more climbing in and out of the bath" adds Kevin. "We love it."

Among the other names on the memorial is Pte William Hemmingway, a Stanley man improbably enlisted in the Argyll and Sutherland Highlanders during the Great War, to whom Kevin has family ties and who died on the Somme on December 21 1915. "He worked down the pit but was terrified so decided to take his chance in France" says Kevin. "He left five bairns behind."

Those on the opposite face include Frank Race, whose mother back on the Hill Top always believed that one day he'd come marching home. Kevin lived nearby as a child. "It was the same every Wednesday night, I was sent round to Susie's fish shop, threepence for going, to get fish and chips twice. She lived alone but the table would always be properly set with two places, best china, fire blazing, everything.

"That poor woman believed until the day she died that their Frank would come back one day. I always wondered who ate the other lot of fish and chips."

The service is simple, thoughtful and dignified. Catherine observes that 2021 is the centenary of the Royal British Legion. "They do so much good. I could spend all morning talking about the Royal British Legion" she says. There are no hymns, no bugler, no standards to lower but some loyally to maintain. Perfectly observed around the memorial, the two-minute silence is accompanied by the clip-clopping of a trotting horse, briskly hauling its cart up Billy Row bank.

Mrs Lawes has another Remembrance service in Satley, where horses are apparently frequent visitors, Richard Manchester, the local Durham County councillor, hopes subsequently to lay a wreath at Thornley at 10am, Billy Row at 11 and to make it up to Tow Law before proceedings conclude there. "It's important" says Richard, "that we never, ever, forget."

The service is over by 9 20am, time for Kevin to recall unhappy days at Stanley school, taught by Bob Marsh, long a popular stalwart of the village cricket team – "as good with the stick as he was with the bat" says Kevin.

His own grandmother, he says, was particularly well known around Stanley – "brought people into the world and laid them out again."

Wooley Terrace was demolished when they were kids. "We'd just play among the wrecked houses, sixpenny sandals from Woolworth's, One day we found a clip of ammunition and one of my mates had the hellish idea to drop a brick on it. He took half his calf off but I think his mother just put some Germolene on. He still has the scars."

This may be the incident reported in a paragraph in The Times in March 1955. "Peter Atkinson, aged 17, an engineer, was seriously hurt yesterday in a mortar bomb explosion on an opencast coal site at Stanley, near Crook, Co Durham, which was used as a mortar training range during the war." It says nothing

War and Peace – the inauguration of Billy Row War Memorial 1921

about Germolene, though.

Kevin also recalls the time they found a great hoard of cash in Wooley Wood – "from a night club in Stockton, I think" – properly informed the polliss but kept some coins for themselves. "We'd use them for skimming on Gents's pond when the frogs were spawning, trying to hit one. I've often thought of buying a deep sea diver's suit. There must be about £50 down there."

Kevin spent 30 years working at Brancepeth Golf Club, a few miles east, recalls controversy in the 1980s when a clubhouse meeting was held to decide if the "working man" should be admitted. "These days they'll let any bugger in" says Kevin, and that's doubtless to their credit.

Another public meeting had been held in Stanley village hall to determine whether to plant a few hardy trees near the war memorial. "People thought there was a better use for the money," says Kevin. "All that fuss for a few blooming trees."

The village, he fears, has changed for the worse. "No pubs, no shops. Shops were where people talked." That seems to me quite profound.

The intention also to attend the 11am service in Billy Row means that there's time for breakfast at the Horse Shoe Inn, the Wetherspoons in Crook. Ten o'clock on the Sabbath and already they're queuing outside Gregg's. Headed with a poppy, a notice in Spoons advises that there'll be a minute's silence at 11am. A flyer announces that, since this is November 14, the Christmas menu will start the following day.

Among the difficulties I have with Wetherspoons, that and the refusal on any account to admit the apostrophe, is the insistence on attaching a calorie count to every dish. The large breakfast comes in at 1,421, Sharon's mushroom benedict still runs to 471. "It must be the hollandaise sauce" she says. Guilt-tripped and replete, we head back up the hill to Billy Row.

The memorial on Billy Row green was unveiled precisely a century ago, November 11 1921. Solemn and formal, there's a grainy picture on the *If you lived at Stanley* Facebook page with one of the pit village's two Methodist chapels in the background.

Each of the memorial's four faces is dedicated to men from a different locality – Billy Row, Grahamsley, Roddymoor and White Lea, though only a local might know where to draw the line.. Most were soldiers, many once again DLI – Poor Bloody Infantry – other regiments again identified by their initials: LNL, EY, MCG, ER. Only a military historian might decipher.

Getting on 100 are gathered on the green, including a group of motor bikers with "Lest we forget" carefully painted on the back of their leathers, and some residents pushed across from the West Lodge care home, nearby.

Some wear the Legion beret, others have chests full of medals, though there's surprising confusion about the side on which they should be worn. There's also a debate over who should lay a wreath. "You're a Nig veteran so you're getting a spamming" a veteran ripostes, esoterically.

Sadly, it's all unsatisfactory, from the misspellings on the photocopied order of service to the announcement at the start that the single hymn – *O God our help in ages past* – won't be sung. "To be honest, why bother?" says the beret wearing leader – he really does. An iffy PA system essays *Last Post, Reveille* and the *National Anthem*. As if it were some sort of arcane local tradition, the silence is again accompanied by the same trotting horse, retracing its steps. They don't even mention the centenary, not the hundred-year war.

There are wreaths, among others, from Peases West school over the road, from the local Neighbourhood Watch, from the Legion and from the South Atlantic Association. The whole thing, including the silence, lasts barely ten minutes. Afterwards there's beer and broth, rumour of corned beef pie, in Billy Row club. Some of us, of course, have already seen off a 1,471 calorie breakfast. We head thankfully for home.

24: death of a warrior

November 15 2021:

Dave Ayre's funeral throngs St Thomas's church, perhaps the biggest gathering of trades unionists in Co Durham since two summers ago when the virus first laid low the Big Meeting.

"An irrepressible, charming man of strong passions" says the Rev Jon Whalley, Vicar of Stanley and neighbouring parishes. "The union became his passion, any injustice became a call to arms to Dave and Doris. Their door was in every sense always open. Dave never turned anyone away."

Heartfelt, Dave Ayre and friend

"An old fashioned sense of compassion coupled with a sharp mind, He was a fixer and, if he couldn't fix it, he knew someone who would" says the Rev Geoff Lawes. He was, adds Mr Lawes, the salt of the earth – "and a phenomenon on a bike."

"A resistance fighter and a good one at that" says Steve Cason, on behalf of the trades unions – to which all of them might have added that Dave was a delightful and, perhaps paradoxically, a gentle man and the best possible to have on your side.

They've come from all over the land, some of them comrades whom Dave met on marches. Solid in death as in life. In the pew behind, a couple of locals are explaining to a visiting Scouser the difficulty of having two places called Stanley and also the pronunciation of "Wooley". They rhyme it with truly.

Dressed for the part, like for Lycra, a few of Dave's former colleagues from Weardale Cycling Club have also pedalled over.

I'd reunited with Dave on July 21, less than a fortnight before his 90th birthday, at the care home in Billy Row to which he and Doris had reluctantly removed. Perhaps his only regret was that West Lodge hadn't an open fire, though his own flame still bright burned. It was to be our last conversation.

Union banners are displayed in the chancel, that of the Crook branch of UCATT – "Socialism and revolution" – at the centre. In front of them, Pam Oliver has bedecked a dusty old bike with flowers – "we kept it dusty, he hadn't used it for two years" – while at the back are his familiar satchel, some of his books and a pair of broken glasses.

"Dave was always breaking his glasses, sat on them usually" says Pam.

St Thomas's, as previously we have recorded, also has a stained glass window dedicated to International Workers' Memorial Day. Few doubt that, but for Dave's efforts, the church would have closed years ago. His own epitaph may be that of Christopher Wren at St Paul's: "If you seek a memorial, look around

you"

I'd known Dave – many called him Davey – for maybe 30 years, since we sat in his little house on the Heights of Alma around the fire that was never allowed to go out. The image, of

Banner man: Dave Ayre

course, was appropriate.

"A helper to many" said the formal death notice in the *Echo*, succinctly, and many of those he helped are gathered to say their farewells. Doris – "deserves a sainthood" says Jon Whalley – arrives in a wheelchair, their dog trots quietly alongside a family member. The cortege enters to Ella Fitzgerald singing Stairway to the Stars. The first hymn's *Jerusalem*, the second *How great thou art* and the third *Fight the good fight*. You wouldn't have got very long odds against that one.

The organ (and the organist) are wonderfully stirring, too. What a loss to the community they would be.

As Dave had done at West Lodge back on that baking July day, Mr Whalley recalls how greatly he had disliked school, the only enjoyable bit being sent with a wheelbarrow to the colliery stables to get manure for the school garden. His father had told him always to pay his union dues and always to pay his rent, added the vicar – and strictly in that order.

Davey, he says, believed that the church was a village asset – "it was worth having if it was only there for one person who sought solace, if only to listen to the birds."

Steve Cason recalls that they'd first met 30 years previously at a meeting to campaign for better local bus services – around the Hill Top he supposes it to have failed – how Davey was old school ("still wrote letters with pen and paper"), how he'd stood solid with the Shrewsbury 24 and how (of course) he detested the Tories.

"We've taken our eyes off the ball, let the Trojan horses in, those Tory MPs. We need to see them out at the next election."

The cortege leaves to the Bob Marley song *Get up, stand up* in which the next few words are "Fight for your rights". David Lewis Ayre fought for them always, and valiantly to the end.

25: the tragedy of Dylan Lee

November 19 2021:

This is different and it's difficult. It's the story of a young man of 19 who hanged himself in particularly distressing circumstances, of the tragedy's aftermath and of what it may say in 2021 about the folk – some of them – who live on the Hill.

Dylan Lee, eldest of six siblings, was found hanged in a shed at the family home in Stanley on Monday May 16 this year. He was a bright lad, conscientious and caring – and he and his family were Gypsies.

"There has been a campaign of ethnic cleansing, it's racially motivated" says Jane Lee, his mother, in the course of a two-and-a-half hour interview. "Ethnic cleansing" is a phrase that none might ever have supposed to hear about that once coal-black village, where all mucked in together.

Jane is 51, articulate, determined and surprisingly self-composed. She has two anthropology-related degrees including a masters in evolutionary medicine, speaks good Italian, is a second dan martial arts black belt and instructor, has worked with primary care trusts and as an education officer with the travelling community, is a parent governor at the village school and a teacher elsewhere. "We have done nothing wrong and we've said nothing wrong" she says. "There has been real hatred, no one should be treated like this."

We talk about the small minority of village people said to have driven Dylan to his death, talk about naked racism in that once-cohesive community, talk about the petition to get the Gypsies out – they even asked her to sign it – and about her campaign to get justice, however posthumously, for her beloved eldest son.

Tragic loss – Dylan Lee

There has, she claims, been stalking, filming, recording of all their movements. Tyre fires have been started with accelerants, rubbish dumped, broken glass left in the chicken run, endangering both the animals and the youngsters as they collected eggs.

Though she names those she believes chiefly to be responsible – imprudent to do so in print – she's grateful for majority support. "The number of village people who came up to me or sent messages after Dylan died has been overwhelming; there's still a community spirit in Stanley."

Mostly she is self-controlled, superficially at any rate – "but if I thought it wouldn't come back on me I'd do them all in" she says, and then swiftly, wisely, reconsiders. "That would fit their stereotype. They'd say that's what Gypsies do. I'm not going to be a stereotype for anyone."

Much of the talk, though, is about Dylan. "Before he hanged himself, he even took his shoes off so he wouldn't leave marks on the stool" says Jane. "It's the kind of boy he was."

Two days after his death, she raised a Gypsy flag on her land – the land where Dylan is buried – and where there's little doubt that it'll blow, bravely, in the wind. It represents total defiance, she says.

Jane was raised on a council estate in Middlesbrough, left school at 16, worked as a seamstress – "mainly for cousins and other family" – and in a Chinese restaurant before deciding at 26, to further her education.

Her father was born in what the Gypsy Romany Traveller community calls a living wagon and was taught properly to read and write only when on National Service. Jane became not just the first family member to gain a degree but the first consistently to attend school.

In 2013 she moved to Deerness Heights, the swish new houses atop Billy Row bank, with her husband and six children – Dylan, Betty who's now 18, Connor who's 17, Gabriel 14, Raphael 13 and 11-year-old Kaziah.

"I'd done my research – I'm an anthropologist, after all – and it seemed fine. We had some lovely neighbours, A few of them had come from other estates in Newton Aycliffe or wherever and looked down on other people in the village because they thought they were better, but mostly they were all right."

After her husband left – "I put him out" says Jane, bluntly – she bought waste land on what locals call the Bomb Hole, behind Francis Street. Chiefly with Dylan's help, it has been levelled and attractively transformed, home to a large chalet and a couple of caravans but also to a polytunnel, a coop of chickens, a stable and an (allegedly) recalcitrant goose. Dylan, says his mum, knew all that there was to be known about chickens (and could handle the goose, as well.)

"It was an eyesore" says Jane. "It was mostly Dylan and me who transformed it. He was pushing wheelbarrows endlessly. Stanley wasn't a culture shock because everything we could do in Middlesbrough we could still do here. I could go back to Middlesbrough tomorrow but times have changed and there are social issues.

"I've seen encampments and I've seen rubbish and stuff left behind but that doesn't mean we're all like that and doesn't mean we're all uncontrollable. I understand the Gypsy policies, understand why not everyone wants to live in the same place all the time but some of the things that are happening are like 1930s Germany."

At the gate, the plot is identified as The Grange. Next to it, another sign says "Welcome". Most, the great majority, were welcoming in turn. Some weren't. Even a police officer, on one of more than 20 occasions that Jane had formally complained of racial harassment or of stalking – by no means all eliciting a constabulary response – told her that he knew they were Gypsies because they had a caravan and a black-and-white horse. "Like I say, I just won't be anyone's stereotype.

"I've always worked, paid for everything I've got, don't owe a penny to anyone in the world – and still people do this. Some of them are just bullies, as if we've something to be ashamed of in being Gypsies. There's nothing to be ashamed of being a Gypsy."

Until ten days before his death, she'd detected no signs that the pressure – the hostility, the peering eyes, the broken glass, the tyre fires, the stalking – was getting to her son.

Dylan was 6ft 2ins tall, bespectacled, quiet but amiable. Like his siblings he neither drank alcohol nor smoked cigarettes and had absolutely nothing to do with drugs. He'd gained A-levels at Wolsingham School, was an outstanding photographer – "did a course, got a distinction star" – created ingenious Lego models and loved the land. University remained an option.

While she was in hospital awaiting his birth Jane contracted sepsis, resulting in peritonitis, a burst appendix and breathing problems. "They put me on two drips and double strength antibiotics, told me that if that didn't work there was nothing else they could do but let me stay with Dylan in the maternity unit.

I just thought to make the most of every day after that.

"We've always been close. He was such a lovely kid, always inquisitive, spoke in sentences from about 18 months old. I always remember watching the news with him during the Iraq crisis and Dylan saying that Tony Blair was a very bad man. I don't think he was two.

"He was always academic, I remember a teacher saying he was very gifted, and his behaviour was just as brilliant. He wasn't a loner, but he chose wisely. He wasn't in your face, not that kind of boy, but he was comfortable in his skin and wanted to be comfortable with those around him. If he didn't like you he wouldn't say anything, he'd just go off somewhere else."

Dylan had been a bit quiet, a bit quieter than usual, in the days before his death. "He knew what was happening but he didn't want trouble and he never caused it, he never even swore" says Jane. "He said he was fine, but he wasn't."

Alone while his mother was at work and his siblings at school, he'd pick up Kaziah from the primary school about half a mile away. Concerns were raised when he didn't. He'd put the hens back in their coop, piled up crates to obscure the shed windows, removed his shoes. When Gabriel found him, emergency services advised him to cut his brother down. Two ambulance crews worked for 45 minutes to try to save him – "they were magnificent" says Jane.

The story made the i newspaper – when last was the Hill Top in the national media? It told of Jane's fight for a second inquest more greatly to take into account the sustained campaign of harassment against the family. "It has been made out to be an ongoing neighbour dispute rather than something that's a one-sided campaign of hatred" she said.

The story also elicited a couple of posts on the village website. "Those individuals should hang their heads in shame," said one. "They should think a thousand shames of themselves" read another.

In the immediate aftermath of Dylan's death, trades unionist and left wing activist Daniel Kebede – partner of former NW Durham MP Laura Pidcock – set up an on-line fund raising page to help the quest for "justice". It was a tragedy that should never have happened, he wrote. The case has been taken up, said the i, by The Good Law Project, a charity. Research claims that Gypsies and travellers are six times more likely to die by suicide than non-travellers, a likelihood increasing to seven times among traveller men.

"People of Gypsy, Roma and Traveller heritage disproportionately experience bullying because of their race" said Jo Maugham, the Good Law Project's director. "It can have a devastating impact on their mental health. Tragically, Dylan could not see a way out."

With a tragic irony, given her heritage, Jane Lee's going nowhere. "There's no way we're leaving, it's not an option. My son's on this land, we brought him back. We're staying here with Dylan."

26: Sunniside up

December 4 2021

Those who wrestled with O-level English may recall the King's great rallying call in *Henry V*: "Once more unto the breach dear friends, once more." It's a bit like that this morning, and without offence to Stanley – or, indeed, to Sunniside, the ultimate destination. It's to do with the No 1 bus.

As chilling to the bones as to the spirits, particularly given the need for Covid ventilation, the No 1 offers little in the way of Christmas cheer. Mind, it would probably be the same if they decked it with Norwegian spruce, festooned it with fairy lights and had the driver dress up as Father Christmas to give out free mince pies.

What the driver does instead is whistle Jingle Bells, a truly cacophonous rendition which resembles a mynah bird in the latter stages of castration, performed without anaesthetic.

The hope, of course, had been to find a little festive spirit on the Hill Top, or at least the part that's home to Stanley Crook. An email to village hall secretary Valerie Singleton brings the swift and civil response that nothing whatever is planned there. Val blames "circumstances."

Sunniside, a mile or so to the west and just as close to heaven, has this very day a Christmas fair, 12-3pm, in the community centre. In the evening at the nearby Moss Inn there's a fund raising quiz and raffle for the still-threatened parish church in Stanley.

Sunniside once had four churches – two Methodist, Cof E and Spiritualist, local lads said to be in the reprehensible habit of sneaking into the basement of the Spiritualist sanctum to knock on the floorboards above. Was anybody there? The effect may only be imagined. The village school closed in the year 2000, its pupils spirited away to Stanley.

Outside the community centre there's a notice about the quiz, the only problem that one of my beer-bottle spectacle lenses has become detached en route from its overstretched frame and that, even more myopic then usual, I take it to read "quiz and rattle" and spend several minutes wondering if the rattle's for the losers to throw out of their pram.

Like Stanley, Sunniside has a namesake within the boundaries of the former County Palatine of Durham. Neither may be particularly appropriately named. The other's near Whickham, south of the Tyne, once home to a celebrated night club called the Blue-something-or-other – Blue Parrot? – owned by Billy

A bit parky – Sunniside

"Tiny" Hutchinson, the pianist and musical arranger on Tyne Tees Television's *One O'Clock Show*.

Probably it goes without saying that Tiny Hutchinson was enormous – 6ft 9ins, it's reckoned.

Like its hilly neighbour, the southern Sunniside was built on coal and once had a much larger population, a dozen or more shops and three or four pubs. Now only the Moss remains – named after the wild moorland out the back. Until a few years

Arty – Julie Ward

ago a second pub was called The Comedian after Bob Ritchie, its landlord, who when not pulling pints was laugh-a-minute on the North-East club circuit.

The community centre in Flag Terrace was converted in the 1978 from four small terraced houses next to the recreation ground and is enthusiastically used. Among the instigators was Sue Ennals, daughter of the Secretary of State for Health and Social Security at the time, who lived with her boyfriend and baby in Gladstone Terrace. "I never really was part of my father's ideology" she said at the time.

When last heard of, Ms Ennals was in Sei Lanka, where the views probably weren't as good but you didn't have to go to bed with two pairs of socks and a hot water bottle, even in July.

On Mondays – Happy Monday, they call it – there's a lunch club for anyone in the village and which boasts a five-star food hygiene rating. On a different occasion the Village Pantry, perhaps a food bank by another name, offers the chance to fill a basket with essentials for £1.

There's a bread making group and a sewing group. Mainly through grants, they raised £30,000 to create a children's playground and another £10,500 to equip an outdoor gym, decidedly fit for purpose.

The Christmas fair has also attracted a visit from a rather dashing Santa Claus, accompanied by an assistant in a onesie. I'm trying to work out what the outfit is meant to represent when Santa himself offers the information that it's Rudolph.

"The red nose is a bit of a giveaway" he adds, gently.

For all that the atmosphere's both warm and warming – a kind

HISTORY OF A VILLAGE

Edited by Julie Ward

Judged by its cover, the Sunniside book

lady on a craft stall even fixes my specs – the only problem seems to be that there are few youngsters. Red cloaked, black booted and white bearded, he sits there like the Santa Claus the Little Boy forgot.

Originally from Gateshead, Elizabeth Mather arrived in Sunniside ten years ago. Claire Ritson, her daughter, is now in the village, too. Claire bears a marked resemblance to her in *The Good Life* – not Penelope Keith, the younger model – and is no less content with her lot. "It's a fantastic village, lovely and caring people" she says.

Elizabeth discovered that the community centre was little used. "I asked if anyone had enquired about grants and to a large extent they hadn't. The paperwork can be a bit of a chew but it's amazing what's out there. We've done really well that way" she says.

A classic case of the familiar North-East adage that shy bairns get nee sweets? "That's exactly what it is" she says.

"It's not just about baking bread or sewing clothes or whatever" says Elizabeth, "it's about bringing people together. This building is ours, it's owned by the village, we have a legacy to continue, just carrying it on for the people who had the vision to create it.

"All right it can snow a bit up here, sometimes four seasons in a day, but even then everyone's looking out for one another, particularly the elderly ones."

Claire also talks of how so many Sunniside folk watch out for one another. "Pretty much as soon as I bought a house here I knew that I wouldn't want to live anywhere else in the world, I absolutely love it. It's the people, isn't it? They've a passion for one another up here, they care."

She's anxious that local communities work together. "People might have tended to keep to their own villages in the past but we need to work with Tow Law, Stanley, even Crook. It's happening, and it's for the benefit of all."

Rose Carr, 84, was born in Gladstone Terrace, Sunniside, and greatly doubts that she'll be going anywhere else now. "I love it here" she says. "It can get bad in winter but you're never really alone. Besides, we're used to a little bit of snow in Sunniside. We're in a bit of a dip and visitors might think the road wasn't too bad, but either side it could be closed."

There, too – more tea – is the Rev Jon Whalley, vicar for the past 12 years of God's good acres for many a square mile around. "This mightn't be a very big village" he says, "but it's got an awfully big heart."

Near the community centre entrance, a carefully worked wall hanging carries a simple message: "Sunniside: on top of the world."

Conceived as a Millennium project, not published until the end of 2006, a carefully researched and wonderfully nostalgic village history was edited and encouraged by Julie Ward who lived in Sunniside, helped form the communities-based and greatly successful Jack Drum Arts company and stood for the European parliament somewhere in the north-west. In 2022 she was "arts lead" for the Commonwealth Games in Birmingham.

Comparisons abound; like Stanley it has perforce changed, though perhaps the approach has been different. Like Stanley the village was labelled Category D and effectively doomed; like Stanley it had a successful football team – albeit only in the Wear Valley Minor League – like Stanley had great long rows of cat-swinging two-up two-downs in which a dozen people might somehow co-exist and, like Stanley, tended to be a bit open to the elements.

History of a village reproduces a *Northern Echo* front page from December 6 1965 in which photographs show Sunniside folks shovelling snow while standing on their roofs and the accompanying story talks of a 40ft drift.

The coal house and the netty were across the back street, of course. The story also tells of an elderly couple, trapped for 40 hours, who were about to burn their furniture for warmth when a neighbour at last tunnelled to the rescue. How they'd addressed more down to earth issues is, perhaps fortunately, not recorded.

Exclamation mark ineluctable, the story is simply headlined "Sunniside!"

On a related matter, Dave Ayre – clearly a polymath – had written a chapter about middens and midden men, known sometimes as midnight men, perhaps because of the nocturnal nature of their noisome but necessary activity.

I pay a fiver for a book, another fiver to guess the weight of the cake, another to guess the name of the teddy bear – Boris, appears not to have been successful – and a fourth for a pocketful of raffle, or possibly rattle, tickets. As the No 1 bus shudders and shivers back towards Darlington, the dark clouds gathering over the Saturday afternoon village are clearly of the meteorological and not the metaphorical sort.

It's been a most enlightening visit: this is Sunniside up.

27: flower power

December 17 2021

Sunniside's football team of the late 1940s included Norman Deacon, a left winger described in some cup final programme notes at the time as "the Dally Duncan of the Wear Valley Junior League."

Douglas Duncan, as few may recall, was a Scottish international outside left who won an FA Cup winner's medal with Derby County in 1946 and managed the Blackburn Rovers team which reached the final in 1960. The nickname, apparently, was because he seemed to have so much time to spend on the ball.

Norman mitigates the comparison. "I had a decent left foot but the problem was that my left foot didn't know what my right foot was doing, and vice-versa" he insists, modestly.

He's now 89, as smart as a Christmas carrot, at the official opening this afternoon of the Winter Wonderland flower festival at St Philip and St James' parish church in Tow Law. A few days earlier, he'd been at Gateshead market at 5 30am, in order to get the best and freshest flowers – pick of the bunch, as it were.

Nationally acclaimed for his flower arranging skills, Norman has been organising festivals at Tow Law church since 1984. This year's has 18 displays, themes ranging from Dancing on Ice to Ding Dong Merrily on High and from Frosty the Snowman to When a Child is Born. One of the arrangements has penguins, another is an any-old-iron reconstruction of the Polar Express. While neither may be strictly scriptural, they get the message, regardless.

None reflects In the Bleak Mid-winter. In Tow Law, that might have been considered a bit too close to home.

The only problem is that Covid again stalks the land, Omicronoligcally and ubiquitously. It's advised that masks are worn in church, condensing spectacles like a tin of Nestle's milk and reducing visibility from precious little to bugger-all. Visitors are invited to spot six half-hidden elves; some of us can hardly spot the altar. It recalls notwithstanding the familiar Christmas-time crossword clue "Subordinate clauses (5)"

"Eeeeh, this is lovely" someone says as they do, approvingly and inarguably, in these parts.

Flower power – Norman Deacon

Outside, where Covid compels, the Salvation Army band plays the season's greatest hits, of which *Joy to the world* is the greatest of all. In the parish hall, next to the wind-blown vicarage which in becoming the first parsonage in the kingdom to have double glazing said something compelling about God's mercy – or that, at least, of the Diocese of Durham - they offer "non-alcoholic" ginger wine, surreptitiously masquerading in bottles labelled *Maisons des Bretons*. It probably doesn't translate as ginger wine, not even in Tow Law.

There, too, is Richard Manchester, assiduous Durham County councillor for the Tow Law and Stanley area, last encountered on Remembrance Day. Richard's a bit worried about his upcoming booster jab. "After the last one I slept for 13 hours" he says.

Much of our chat's off the record. What's not is that he hopes

Lighting up time, Christmas trees in Stanley

to persuade the council to provide allotments in Stanley – "just the thing for bringing people together." He thinks that it may have become a commuter village or possibly a computer village. Neither would do much for face-to-face fellowship.

Inside, everything's warm, convivial, invigorating as a bottle of *Maisons des Bretons* best. Outside on a moonlit evening frost lies thick on the ground. It's 4 15pm and I decide to walk the three miles eastward along Windy Ridge to Stanley.

As has become customary, I talk of Stanley Hill Top; Norman Deacon's delighted. "I hate it when people say Stanley Crook, it's not natural" he says, fraternally.

However chilly, it's a lovely winter evening. Crook and places several miles to the south seem to be shimmering, lucky-Jimmering, in the moonlight. Hundreds of yards of five-rail fencing that previously has bordered Sunniside and Stanley Moss lies alongside the verge, flattened a few weeks earlier by Storm Arwen. Every third vehicle which passes seems to be from Sainsbury's, or Tesco, or some such corporation, quietly running for home.

Along the way there's a mystery. On every street in Tow Law, occasionally in Sunniside and in a little row in Stanley, seemingly symmetrical Christmas trees – fixed by brackets (if not parantheses) - protrude at the same upward angle from the upper floors of mainly terraced houses, like a semaphore signal giving the right-away to the Santa Claus Special.

Save perhaps for Buckingham Palace, I can think of nowhere else like it. Has some super-salesman flogged the local community a job lot? Is it some sort of Masonic ritual, reflecting Tow Law's long fascination with the Craft? Have they counted the trees in Hamsterley Forest of late?

Tow Law also has a large and rather handsome community Christmas tree; the centre of Crook's lit up like Blackpool on Bonfire Night. Stanley, poor old Stanley, has nowt.

Many households, particularly on the newish and posh-ish Deerness Heights, have made commendable efforts. Above average, anyway. Wooley Mews, leading (it says) to St Thomas's Court and Tanners Mews) is less lustrous. Some of the long terraces of Mount Pleasant and Francis Street are done out bravely, like the Cratchit family (them again) on Christmas Day. One or two display "Santa stop here" notices. One of them had it up in October.

Perhaps the jolliest of all is a bungalow on High Road, on the way to the old United football ground, the owner clearly bent single-handedly on illuminating the Black Path.

Alone in the festive bar of the Foresters, I learn from the barmaid that Jim Mulligan, the landlord, has taken to his sickbed – though not, happily, from Covid – book us in for New Year's Eve dinner and wonder which is colder, Stanley or Tow Law.

"Tow Law every time" says the barmaid. "No comparison."

The bar of Billy Row Club, without sign of festive frivolity, is slowly filling up. I report that Jim Mulligan's out of fettle. "Must have dropped his wallet on his foot" says someone, unsympathetically.

Trevor Smith reckons that New Year's Eve will be just like any other Friday. It's New Year's Day that's big on the Hill Top, he says. It's New Year's Eve, not quite coincidentally, that will mark nine months since first we ventured beyond lockdown's

limits – remember *The Wind in the Willows?* – up the A68 to Stanley.

It marks the end of an appropriate nine-month gestation period, though whether a bonny bouncing book will result remains – of course – to be seen.

28: Fred letter day

December 21 2021

The Christmas concert at St Thomas's, again the Esh and Bear-park Colliery Band and the Crook and Weardale Singers, was to have been a festive highlight amid December's encircling gloom. Covid, resurgent, sabotages it.

The decision, tripartite, is clearly the correct one but does nothing to enhance the church's prospects of remaining open. Still they talk of a final service at Easter 2022, and with little obvious hope of resurrection.

Nor do two brief paragraphs amount to much of a chapter, not even on the shortest day. It's by wondrous good fortune, therefore – what long-wordsmiths like to call serendipity – that there's an email this afternoon from Fred Ramshaw, for little other reason than to offer compliments of the season and to wonder what I'm up to.

Fred's an old acquaintance, retired teacher, rarely encountered though he lives in the next North Yorkshire village to us, just three miles away. These days he's much involved with the North East Locomotive Preservation Group whose engines he drove until recently and whose shed includes a glorious apple green tank engine called Joem, 69023, once the station pilot at Newcastle Central and latterly, wondrously, restored.

Probably Joem never worked Wooley pit, nor even shunted empties at Bankfoot coke works, the ugly duckling now so beauteous a creature that, were there the least prospect of an affirmative answer, I'd probably propose holy matrimony to her.

Might it even be an excuse to include a winsome photograph – may a steam engine be supposed winsome? – and no matter

Steam up – Fred Ramshaw

154

that poor old 69023 lies at the time of writing in bits on a workshop floor, and with no guarantee that she might survive the ongoing major surgery?

At any rate, the Christmas message to Fred is that I'm trying to write a book on Stanley Hill Top, imagining that he may barely have heard of the place or, worse, suppose that it's a biggish town in Derwentside that may or may not have a swingers' club. "Heard of it?" he replies. "I was brought up there."

A few memories, perhaps? His response is so vivid, so richly redolent of vanished times and of good old bad old days, that it's produced below without editing. Should *Prairie Stories* materialise, I might even give him a copy – though swear him to secrecy, of course.

"We moved from Waterhouses to Stanley just before the Queen's coronation in June 1953, when my dad – a hewer at the coalface – progressed to being a deputy. It was a move which enabled me to collect two commemorative Coronation mugs, though quite a culture shock to come from a junior school in a sheltered valley to one situated on the edge of a village and in the full blast of freezing north-east winds straight from the steppes of Russia. Those kids still in short trousers had almost permanently chapped knees.

"As far as memory serves, each classroom had its own pot bellied coke-fired stove in the corner of the room, protected by very substantial wire mesh fireguards which in the winter were always festooned with clothes being dried before the next battle with the elements.

"Mr Challenger was my teacher, whose ploy to get us to learn poetry was to allow us to leave a few minutes early as soon as we could stand in front of the class and recite a given piece.

"St Thomas's church hall was situated on the other end of the village, overlooking Crook, and most Friday evenings hosted the village youth club – not particularly well organised, as far as I remember, but a popular meeting place.

"Strange as it may seem, inside the hall was a trapeze – a magnet for the boys to try to impress the girls with deeds of skill and daring. Needless to say the girls took no notice as they were more concerned about who was the more popular, Elvis Presley or Cliff Richard. All things being equal, it was usually possible to 'walk a girl home' at the end of the night.

"I lived in Francis Street, so called 'officials' houses for the local colliery. Despite their grandiose standing they were like most houses in Stanley, with an earth closet – the netty – across the yard. These netties needed regularly cleaning out and you very soon learned the times and dates for cleaning as you could easily be caught with your pants down. I had three specific jobs:

1. After heavy snow to dig a path to the toilet across the yard.

2. Light the fire in the wash house every Monday morning – washing day.

3. When the concessionary coal was delivered, shovel it into the coalhouse.

"I well remember the annual club trips to South Shields or Redcar with the men in suits and flat caps and women in their Sunday best hiring deck chairs and tents on the beach with the obligatory jug of hot water to wash down sand-filled cheese sandwiches. After dinner, the men would retire to the local workmen's club while the women took the children to the amusements.

"Stanley had a good selection of shops, making it almost self-contained. My favourite was Susie's fish shop where in exchange for a bundle of newspapers (to wrap up the meal) you could have a free bag of chips, with scrapings. Charlie Wightman, the butcher, had a slaughterhouse out the back. I can still an animal being led through the door, still see the look of terror on its face. It wasn't very nice.

"Then there was a farmer at the Oakenshaw end of the village who always seemed to move his animals at night, I don't know why. We called them the Midnight Farmers.

"Pigeon racing was very popular and I recall on the day of a big race men sitting outside their crees with us peering anxiously into the sky looking for their homing birds. The leek shows were also legendary.

"Stanley United Football Club was an important part of village life. I can well remember large crowds filling the streets while walking to the ground. Us kids had our own personal entrance, bypassing the inconvenience of turnstiles and queues. Jack Lyle

Old favourite: Joem

provided the match entertainment, berating the unfortunate referee in a voice that could be heard in Crook. I do remember the excitement Geoff Strong caused when he played for the Nops.

"After Alderman Cape secondary school in Crook, where I captained the football team, I went to the sixth form at Wolsingham Grammar School and then the early 60s deserted Stanley to start a three-year physical education teacher training course in Winchester. There was never a chance of me following my dad down the pit. He took me down once, illegally, and it was a definite case of 'never again.' That was maybe the intention.

"Returning to Stanley, it was painfully obvious that the Category D label was sticking. The place was being run down and rumours about Wooley colliery closing due to a massive fault making it uneconomic to work – in favour of the easily worked coastal pits – added to the feeling. The shops were gradually closing, as were the pubs. The future of the village and the surrounding area was looking grim.

"When back in the area these days, I often visit the Hill Top to relive old times and am always surprised and heartened by the changing face of the village. Despite signs still remaining of a previous administration the place has a positive attitude, with owner occupied houses all well kept. Along with recent developments, there's a new reason to be there. The old ethos has gone but a new one is thriving.

"Back at Winchester I'd tell the southerners what a horrible, inhospitable place the North-East was and best to be avoided. In fact, I guarded my *Auckland Chronicle* with a passion, in case they discovered the true spirit of the North-East – a spirit found in abundance in a village called Stanley Hill Top."

29: auld acquaintance

December 31 2021:

It's not just on the Hill Top, of course, that New Year is old hat, where first foot is second-rate and where auld acquaintance is pretty much forgotten.

Take Witton Park, the most vaunted of all Co Durham's former Category D villages, a few hilly miles to the south. "You nearly had to have a rota for all the first footing" recalls Doug Belton (who just happens to be enjoying a Hogmanay supper on an almost balmy evening at the Foresters in Stanley.) Balmy? It must be getting on six degrees.

Some bright new years, says Doug, he might start at Mrs Stobart's – "then maybe to Connie's mother's, then my cousin Alan, then my cousin Eric, then off on our rounds. Goodness knows what time we got to bed."

Demand increased, Doug adds, if you were tall, dark and handsome – "sometimes I might be first footing as far off as Escomb." Escomb and its Saxon church must be getting on half a mile away.

Two or three more tables are taken in the Foresters' restaurant, though the three couples booked overnight have all called off because of continuing Covid concerns. Omicron accelerates. Christmas past, the music machine plays *Saving the best till last*, that rather winsome hit – may a song, like a steam engine, be supposed winsome? – for Vanessa Williams.

Guest house owner Jim Mulligan, back on his feet, also remembers happy days of first foot forward. You'd carry a roundy, he says – by which miners meant a great big lump of coal – to chuck on the fire back for good luck. "You weren't always the first foot, of course, but if there was a light on, you just knocked on the door and went in."

Tonight, he says, he doubts if he'll be up beyond 11 o'clock, much less midnight, afoot again for seven and no matter that there'll be no guest breakfasts to prepare. A middle-aged woman takes away two pint bottles of a falling-down beer called Champion, 7.3 per cent, because she'd enjoyed it with her dinner. "Aye" they say in the bar, "she'll be champion in the morning, an'all."

Jim, ever hospitable, again reminds us that he has neither computer nor mobile phone – "plenty of them without me having one" – and is disconcerted when his stapler starts playing silly beggars. "See" he says, "technology."

Sharon's also there, bless her, and wearing her best sparkly Hogmanay jumper, £10 from Sainsbury's. Entreaties that I should one-last-time have come up on the No 1 bus have been rejected in favour of the mucky white car across the road. Auld Lang Syne's one thing, the No 1 from Darlington's probably best forgotten. Everything on the menu's under a tenner. I see out 2021 with leek pudding, mince and tatties, as close to the Scottish model as may be possible. Oor Wullie, if not their Nicola, would be proud.

Geoff Hodgson, Doug Belton's son-in-law, was born in Stanley in 1966 and has moved about a fair bit since then, though never more than a couple of hundred yards from the parental home in Chapel Street. "Why would I want to?" he asks.

"We shifted to Black Road, then Mount Pleasant, then High Road on the way to the football ground. The first time we had a Peugeot 205 and I think we moved everything in that, the others we maybe had a bogey. I never really thought about going anywhere else. Anyway, it's a bit late now."

As he grew up, next to his grandparents' fish shop, they were pulling Stanley's long terraces down. "There was one lady in Wooley Terrace wouldn't go, they knocked the rest down around her. It's different now, the only time I really speak to anyone is when I'm walking the dog. You don't really know the people, but you recognise their dogs."

He also remembers doing a Sunday morning paper round, by no means so ponderous an affair as might these days be imagined but weighty enough when New Year's Day fell on the Sabbath. "Every house you'd get asked in for a glass of sherry and a bit cake. I was only about 12 and I didn't get home till dinner time, absolutely hammered."

The family party leaves shortly after 10pm, no thought of midnight marauding. "We've a bottle of Japanese whisky at home" says Geoff. "I doubt if I'll see nine o'clock Wednesday morning, never mind tomorrow.

We leave at 10 30pm to raise a quick glass at Billy Row club. Whether contemporary custom or Covid caution, not a soul stirs on the streets of Stanley. The Foresters probably won't see another person all night.

Maybe 25, five of them women, are scattered round the club, though as the clock sidles towards 12 the place becomes emptier, not more crowded. Sharon, for whom it's a first visit, notices at once that they have well-used UKIP beer mats, promoting a points-based immigration system and "standing up" for pubs.

Trevor Smith recalls livelier – if not necessarily happier – New Years at the club, though with the proviso that he missed a number of them for the very good reason that he was barred for life, or *sine died* as they used to say within the jurisdiction of the Durham County Club and Institute Union. Something to do with the fruit machine, apparently.

"On New Year's Eve they'd be queuing up and down the bank, both ways" he recalls. "If you weren't in by six o'clock you'd never get in; when the pit was going people always seemed to have a few bob. I don't even know if they always had turns, but all I can remember is that it used to be wild, really wild. There'd be a bloke running round with nothing on and it was only nine o'clock. My dad was nicknamed Fiery Jack; I think he had some good New Years in here, too, living up to his name."

We leave the Hill Top about 11pm, maybe 15 left enthusiastically to wish one another all the best. Quite soon Spring will be in the air, the Mole will again cry "Bother" and "Oh blow" and once more the nation will seek signs of a true end to the wretched pandemic. For the moment we're home just before the bells, wistfully wondering where the past nine months (never mind the last year) have gone, saving the best till last.

Epilogue

Two things became apparent in the course of writing *Prairie Stories*. The first was that Stanley Hill Top could serve as a microcosm of the changing face (and changing fortunes) of so many former pit villages in Co Durham, especially the smaller ones inland.

The second was that if I had a tenner for every time I cack-handedly typed "Staley" and meant "Stanley" – hundreds, literally – I'd be able to afford one of those posh pads on Jobson Meadows.

If not the contagion which elsewhere it became, Covid also proved ineluctable, even compelling the closure – number up – of the firm which printed all those billions of bingo books. I also became a bit over-familiar with the No 1 bus. The 20 miles from Darlington consume an awful lot of time (and this one, let it be noted, is the "express.") Thank goodness for the bus pass.

The intention was to write a chronicle not to draw conclusions, roughly to sketch a history not to lecture on it. What's unavoidable, however, is that Durham County Council's wretchedly ill-conceived Category D policy adversely affected Stanley and so many more happy and close-knit communities – by no means the only catalyst for change but that and colliery closure perhaps the principal ones.

Back in 1990 the county council would have closed the primary school, too, and what a disaster that would have been. On the edge of the village but clearly a centre of excellence, it has become the chief reason why some families have moved to Stanley and perhaps the chief reason that the village survives.

Topics recur: the Little House and the football club which ignited the love affair, the threatened parish church which may have said its last Amen by the time the book appears, the life and death of the incomparably compassionate Dave Ayre, the Big Brother 20 miles to the north. There've also been unexpected sadnesses, not least the tragedy of Dylan Lee, to which a melancholy chapter is devoted.

Nor will I ever again hear Kenny Rogers sing *The Gambler* without picturing that lonesome roadside bench on the way out to Waterhouses. You've got to know when to hold 'em, know when to fold 'em....

A bit like the Prayer Book wedding service, which talks of forsaking all other and keeping thee only unto him – or, doubtless, her – the original thought was to write of Stanley in isolation, to the exclusion of the neighbouring villages, even Billy Row to which it is almost umbilically linked. It would have been unwise and, in any event, impossible. What of all those Brown Ales in Billy Row club? What of the Christmas tree festival in Tow Law or the eye-opener in Sunniside, where community cohesion seems much more evident.

I never really thought that over the nine month gestation period that many on the Hill Top particularly took to me, which is not to say that they took against me. It is blessed with glorious views (weather permitting) and with lovely walks but seems almost to be introverted, a community which these days keeps itself to itself and where the chief opportunity for social interaction is walking the dog.

I'm hugely grateful, nonetheless, to all those who've helped, who welcomed me into their homes and into their community, shared their thoughts and their memories, let me ride a hobby horse, not flog a dead one, and once more be a journalist. It's invidious to pick out individuals, lest some be forgotten, but particular thanks to Ray Ion for his research, to Karl Utley for his time and advice, to his Facebook colleagues for permission to raid their archives and to John Maugham for his splendid images of Stanley primary school and its pupils.

I'll leave the Hill Top alone now, leave it to mind its own business and to contemplate its own future. It's different, it's fascinating and I'm thankful for the opportunity to have got feet beneath its table, and in getting to know it better to appreciate it yet more.

Index

Figures relate to chapters

BELL George 1

BELL John 9

BELLAMY David 2

BELTON Doug 29

BILL and BEN, the Flowerpot Men 1,8

BLAIR, Sir Tony 3, 25

BLENKIRON Billy   10

BOWMAN Ian 13

BRADLEY Gordon 10

BROOKS William 9

BROONS The 8

BROWN Alan 16

BROWN Cherry 10

BROWN Gordon MP 4

BROWN Porky 10

BROWN-HUMES J E 21

BURN Keith 10

BURKE Paddy 10

BUTTON Family 5

BUTTON Martin 21

CARR Rose 26

CARSWELL Christian Michael 7

CASON Steve 24

CHARLTON Janet 20

CHRISTIE David 7, 19

CHRISTIE Holly 19

CHUCKLE BROTHERS, Barry and Paul Elliott 21

CLARK Mary Jane 1

CLARK Wayne 6,7

CLARKE Harry 10

CLINTON Hillary 17

CLOUGH Brian 10

COATES PC 18

COMFORT Dr Alex 13

CORNER Nick 6

CORRIGAN Dr Paul 3

COWANS Frank 15

CRAGGS Dawn 8

CRAGGS Tommy 7

CRATCHETT Bob 20

CROMWELL Oliver 6

CRONIN Paddy 7

CUMMINGS Dominic 5

CUMMINGS Tommy 4,10

DAVIS Fr Peter 1,11

DAVISON Lynn 8

DEACON Norman 27

DOLAN Ian10

DUNCAN Dally 27

ELWELL Paul 7

ENNALS Sue 7

FIELD Bob 6

FITZGERALD Ella 24

FLINTSTONE FRED 7

FOREVER FRIENDS 18

FRENCH Narinda 15

FRENCH Paul 15

GAGARIN Yuri 13

GIBSON Rev Granville 9

GRAHAME Kenneth 1

HANCOCK Tony 13

HARRISON Maj Gen 6

HAYDON Thomas 9

HELEN, Princess of Romania 22

HEMMINGWAY Pte William 23

HESLOP Kevin 23

HILTON Cuthbert 5

HODGSON Geoff 29

HODGSON Harry 15

HOGAN Frank 10,15,20

HOLDEN Richard MP 4,19

HOLLOWAY Stanley 3

HOLMES Sherlock 17,18

HOOD J 5,14

HOOD Robin 12

HOPE Joan 21

HOPE Shaun 19,21, 22

HOPPER Graham 7

HORN Tommy 10,11

HUGHES Hilton 9

HURLEY Charlie 3

HUSSEIN King of Jordan 13

HUTCHINSON Billy 26

ION Ray 1,11,14

IRVINE Marie 7

JENKINS Dr David 2, 11 20

JOBSON Doreen 10

JOEM 28

JOHNSON Barry 20

JOHNSON Boris 9

JOHNSON Evelyn 20

JOHNSON Samuel 5

JONES Joey 16

JUAN CARLOS King 13

KEBEDE Daniel 25

KEEGAN Kevin 17

KERRIDGE Dan 4

KINDLEYSIDES Jonathan 2,11 12

KING Dr Martin Luther 11

KIRKUP Vince 1,10

ROUGHLEY Billy 10

ROW Sir William 4

ROWLING J K   19, 23

RUTHERFORD Dave 10

RYDER Vera 12,23

SANTA CLAUS 26

SHARRATT Harry 10

SHEARER Alan 15

SHOULDER Alan 10

SIMON and GARFUNKEL 12

SIMPSON Albert 7

SIMPSON Sarah Ann 21

SINGLETON Valerie 7,26

SMART Dickie and Norman 10

SMITH Francis 10

SMITH John MP 3

SMITH Trevor 4, 15, 16, 27,29

SOWERBY Doris 18

SPENCE Billy 18

SPENCE Eleanor 18

STEPHENSON Joe 14

STOBBS Allan 5,6

STOKER Ernie 9

STRONG Geoff 10, 28

SWINBANK David 18

TAIT Phil   20

TAYLOR June 7

TAYLORSON Titchy 9

THATCHER Margaret 2, 4,13

THEAKER Billy 10

THOMPSON Bobby 10

THOMPSON Edward 7

THURSBY Bob   10

TINKLER Cyril 22